The Mary Foundation
PO Box 26101, Fairview Park, OH 44126
www.catholicity.com

The Warning
The Concise Revised Edition

The Scripture texts used in this work are taken from **The New American Bible,** Revised Edition © 2011 by the Confraternity of Christian Doctrine, Washington, DC. Some names have been changed to protect the privacy of individuals. Queen of Peace Media and the Mary Foundation assume no liability for damages that may result from the use of information contained herein.

IMPRIMATUR
✠ Ramón C. Argüelles, STL
Archbishop Emeritus of Lipa, Philippines
May 22, 2020

Library of Congress Control Number: 2020920923

ISBN-10: 0964631687
ISBN-13: 9780964631687

Cover design by Bud Macfarlane
Typesetting by Joe Vantaggi of Impressions Printing
Printed in the United States of America

Table of Contents

THE WARNING
CONCISE REVISED EDITION

CHRISTINE WATKINS

AS EDITED AND SUPPLEMENTED BY

BUD MACFARLANE
XAVIER MACFARLANE

The Mary Foundation
Rocky River • Ohio • USA

Foreword

You are about to read true stories by real people from all walks of life. They will transform how you perceive the world and your place in it.

The event each contributor experienced is known as an illumination of conscience. Many individuals from all over the world have undergone uncannily similar incidents. At the end of this book, you will discover how, when, and why this will occur simultaneously to every person on earth.

This little book found its way into your hands today for a reason, just as it found its way into ours. While preparing it for publication, we were surprised to find ourselves in these stories. You are in here, too. Find yourself.

Bud Macfarlane
Xavier Macfarlane
Editors of the Concise Revised Edition

December 8, 2020

Alan Ames

In 1993, I traveled frequently for my job as a sales manager for a pharmaceutical company in the city of Perth, Australia. During one trip, when I was forty, I flew to Adelaide and went through my monotonous routine of checking into to a hotel and sitting on the bed to watch television. Though normally a heavy drinker, I hadn't downed any booze because I didn't generally consume alcohol on a work day.

While I was watching the evening news, all the sudden, directly in front of me appeared a horrific-looking man who reached his arms forward and began to choke me. He had dark skin and bulging eyes, with lips drawn back into a snarl that exposed his ghastly teeth—but I was less concerned with his appearance than the fact that he was strangling me!

I tried to use my martial arts moves against him, having been the captain of the Australian team in the Aikido World Championships, but my hands passed right through his body. Nothing I could do would stop his stranglehold.

Following several minutes of useless struggling, the veins in my neck were about to burst, and I believed I was taking my very last breath.

Then an audible voice in my head said, "Pray the Our Father!" That was the last idea I would have come up with, but in desperation, I started to pray it, and the strangling stopped.

Then I stopped praying and the strangling resumed. Every time I ceased to pray, the strangling started, and every time I resumed, the strangling stopped. To add to this nightmare, I was trapped and couldn't move. I tried repeatedly to get out of the hotel room, but the terrifying man kept me pinned in a stranglehold—and this went on all night.

The experience was so strange and frightening that I thought I'd gone mad. *That's it. I'm absolutely crazy.* I'd heard of people who drank in excess and would see pink elephants traveling up the wall, so I figured I was one of them.

Then I saw my neck in the hotel mirror. To my amazement, it was bruised; therefore, I couldn't deny the attack was real. Yet I couldn't accept it either.

The next day, I heard the same voice in my head that had told me to pray the Our Father. He told me he was an angel whom God had sent to help me. I didn't believe in the existence of angels. They were nothing more than make-believe fairies. He said God had sent him because God loved me and wanted my love.

"If God exists," I answered back to this fairy in my head, "surely He wouldn't love someone like me!"

I had good reason to think I was a poor candidate for love. God had always been the furthest thought from my mind, and troublemaking the first. I was born on November 9, 1953, in Bedford, England, north of London, to an English dad and an Irish-Catholic mum from County Kerry.

She was often praying the Rosary, attending church, and trying to bring me up in the faith, but I had no interest in religion whatsoever. Ignoring her efforts completely, I preferred to leave the house in order to play and steal money, causing my mum multiple heartaches. Coming from a poor family, I was hateful toward those who had toys, who had holidays, who had things I couldn't have.

Even from a very early age, I didn't believe God was real. Perhaps a group of wise men had gotten together and jotted down guidelines on how we should live without hurting each other, and wrapped it up in this story called Jesus.

At age twelve, I started drinking alcohol and was brought before a court judge for taking money out of the candle box in Saint Edmund's Church in Edmonton, London.

At age fourteen, I had the worst record of all the students at a Jesuit school in Stamford Hill, and was finally expelled for stealing.

I felt the only way I was going to get treated with any dignity was to follow in the footsteps of my own father: an aggressive, alcoholic gambler. People were frightened of him and gave him a grudging respect, which he gained through violence. I copied his habits, including his constant drinking, because alcohol gave me good feelings and numbed me to all the bad things in my life. But the next day would always come, when everything felt worse, so I would drink again to drown the consequences.

I grew up in a dangerous part of London with my parents and my four brothers. In my teen years, I joined a motorcycle gang and became extremely violent. Most of my friends were like myself: thugs and thieves. My best friend killed someone, another friend was murdered at the age of seventeen, another was blinded while fighting, and another attempted to murder an older woman.

I learned Aikido because at 5 feet, 7 inches tall, I realized there were a lot of men out there much bigger than I. When a man who had been protecting me was put in prison for twelve years for murder, I worked hard to better protect myself and eventually achieved a fourth-degree black belt, later becoming captain of the Australian team in the 1992 World Championships in Tokyo. I had a very bad temper, and the martial arts taught me how to use it to harm people: break their bones, punch them, kick them, and even kill them. I hurt others out of jealousy because they seemed to have what I didn't—money and the love of a happy family.

At age eighteen, I ran into my Australian wife-to-be and covered up my real self so she would like me. She noticed me drinking a lot but didn't realize I was addicted to the stuff. She must have loved me. She married me.

We lived in London, and life was hard for me there as an uneducated, struggling warehouse worker, so my wife said, "Let's go to Australia. Life is better there."

I agreed, and we moved to Perth in 1976.

Several years later, I managed to obtain my job with the pharmaceutical company by lying in order to get the position. To keep the job, I had to actually study the topic of medicine, and my learning paid off because I stayed there for ten years, rising to sales manager. It was a great job, an easy job, which paid lots of money and provided plenty of opportunities for raising Cain.

Drinking is very popular in Australia, and I fit in quite well. Outside of work, much of my life revolved around carousing, fighting, stealing, swindling, and lying.

The only thing I didn't do was murder, but I came frighteningly close to it a few times. I lived for power, money, and a good time at all times. But suffering always dragged down my dreams because my pleasure came from addictions and sin, with their lingering imprint of pain, hurt, loneliness, and emptiness.

My life was a dark one when the angel I mentioned started to visit me. Even when I heard his voice, I still didn't believe that he existed, so I said to him, "Prove you are real."

And he did. He started to tell me of different things that would happen in my life, which I shared with my wife—and to our amazement, they all came true.

The angel was gentle, but I didn't listen to him; therefore, in his stead, God sent in the big guns. One night, when I was again in the city of Adelaide, but staying in a different hotel, Saint Teresa of Avila appeared in my room. (I later discovered she is a sixteenth century Catholic saint from Spain.)

Her face looked hawkish and stern, that of a strict school teacher, and she was wearing a brown Carmelite habit. She proceeded to give me a kick up the back side, saying I needed to change my life completely to avoid going to hell, which she then described in frightening detail.

That woke me up. Before then, hell was only a made-up myth to trick people into living better, but now, if that place existed, I certainly didn't want to go there. Saint Teresa explained to me that I had to start loving God and my fellow men. Each person, she said, is created in the image of God, and to love Him would naturally mean to love other people, regardless of their differences or behavior toward me. Then she revealed what could be mine: she told me about heaven.

"That is where I want to go!" I cried.

"You can reach paradise," she said to me, "Anyone can. If you live your Catholic faith, you are guaranteed heaven."

She insisted, "Pray, pray the Rosary!"

Then she asked me to go get one.

I didn't want to pray. Prayer was boring, so I looked for excuses. "Where can I get rosary beads at this time of night?"

"There is a shop around the corner that is open and sells rosary beads."

"At 9:30 at night? That's impossible!"

"You go there!" She ordered.

This is totally nuts, I thought as I walked outside. Turning the corner, I saw a religious shop. It was open, and they were stocking inventory. Saint Teresa directed me downstairs where many rosaries were on display. I couldn't believe it. She showed me a brown rosary, which I later discovered was the color of the Carmelite order to which she belonged.

"Get that one," Saint Teresa urged.

Rosary beads in hand, I returned the hotel room. Standing in front of her, I resumed my litany of excuses: "I can't pray this," or "There are so many prayers, there are too many Hail Marys and Our Fathers."

Each night, as an insurance policy, I had been in the habit of saying ten seconds of prayer. I figured if I died in my sleep, God would take me to heaven—that is, if it existed.

"Pray the Rosary," Saint Teresa insisted, "and pray fifteen decades!" That equals three entire Rosaries.

"Ugh." I didn't like prayer, so I started a giant argument with Saint Teresa.

"You must pray," she kept on. "You must pray the Rosary because you risk losing your soul! Unless you change, you're going to hell."

Needless to say, she won the argument.

I didn't really know the Rosary, so she explained how to pray it. She said that I should see it as a window into the life of God on earth, that I should place myself beside Jesus and walk with him through his life. By doing so, his grace would reach inside of me and touch me in a powerful way.

"Every prayer of the Rosary," she told me, "is a step away from evil and a step toward God. See the Rosary as a chain you are hanging around the neck of Satan, which will weigh him down and break his grasp on you."

From my first Rosary prayer, I felt a peace, a happiness, an excitement within. I couldn't stop laughing, and I couldn't stop crying. No drug or alcohol could have given me what I was feeling at that moment. The more I prayed, the stronger this became, until suddenly, I had finished fifteen decades. I wanted to continue.

"Why is this happening?" I asked Saint Teresa. "When I see other people praying, they often have long faces and look miserable, as if they were forced to pray. Yet this is really joyful, wonderful stuff. Don't other people experience what I'm experiencing in prayer?"

"Well, often they don't," she answered, "because so often when they pray, they're thinking about themselves. They're focusing on their lives, their problems, their concerns. When you focus on self, God gets pushed aside. When God comes second, and self is first, your heart actually starts to close to God and stops his grace from filling you.

"However, when you focus on God in your prayers and look past yourself, past the world, that is when your soul opens. God pours his grace in abundance deep inside you."

She said to tell people that when they begin to pray, the first thing they should do is turn to the Holy Spirit and say:

"Lord, I can't pray properly. I'm weak. I'm human. I'm fragile. I'm easily distracted, taken into thoughts of myself and the world. But you, Lord, lead me past that. Help me to pray properly. Help me to focus on the Father, the Son, and You, Holy Spirit, so that my soul can be opened, and I can receive the grace that is there for everyone in prayer."

She continued, "Once you do that, once you seek God's help in prayer and in all you do, you can start to experience what prayer is meant to be: a joyful gift of God's love.

"If prayer is a burden, a chore, a duty, this is often because prayer is self-centered and not God-centered. Remember, in all things God must come first. Look to God in everything, and then you will receive His joy in all you do."

From the moment I started to pray the Rosary, Satan's grasp on me weakened. My addictions fell away, and I had many of them, alcohol being the primary one. This is nothing I did, but a grace from God. Anyone who has been addicted to alcohol knows how hard it is to quit, and I quit immediately.

In moments of temptation, when I felt weak and so alone, hurt, rejected, and unloved, I was freed and strengthened by remembering Saint Teresa's words to me: "Every time you feel a desire to do wrong, think of Jesus. Just think of his Name, think of him suffering on the Cross, or see the Host before you. Keep concentrating on that and you will see your desires fall away."

Soon after Saint Teresa paid me a visit, other saints came to speak to me. The first were Saint Stephen, Saint Andrew, and Saint Matthew, who encouraged me to read Holy Scripture, which I did. When I went back to England for a holiday, they directed me to walk into Saint Edmund's Church, the same church where I had been caught stealing as a child.

I ended up staying for Mass, which was unusual for me at the time. Afterward, when I knelt and prayed in front of a Sacred Heart of Jesus statue, it suddenly began emanating a white light and came physically alive before my startled eyes.

Then the statue was transformed into the Blessed Mother dressed in white, with light shining forth from within her. So much love was in her smile. Her beauty defied words.

How can I adequately describe her? Her eyes were blue and her hair black. She may have been my wife's height, about five feet, six inches. But this says little. I could see her heart circled in white roses and superimposed on Jesus's Sacred Heart. Never had I heard about the Immaculate Heart of Mary, and only the next day, from a prayer card, did I realize what I had seen: their two Hearts as One.

I was further stunned when Blessed Mother Mary began speaking to me from the living statue. Her first words were, "Pray, pray, pray."

In my flustered and flawed logic, that meant increasing my Rosary prayers by three times, so I began to say numerous decades of the Rosary, every day. Mary also told me she was my mother and that God has given her a wonderful grace to bring people deeper into the Heart of Jesus. From that point on, she would visit me and do just that.

In 1994, Blessed Mother Mary said to me one day, "My Son is coming to you," and before me was Jesus on the Cross, telling me he loved me and he wanted to forgive me. It was the greatest day in my life, but it was also the most difficult because I was shown how all my sins, from childhood to the present, had contributed to his suffering and dying. There were so many of them! It seemed as though I was sinning every second of my life.

I saw how every time I hurt someone, I was hurting Jesus. Any time I told a lie, I was lying about Jesus as he suffered and died. Every time I gossiped about people, I was below the Cross with those gossiping about Jesus as he hung in agony. Any time I made fun of others, I was making fun of Jesus as he died for me. Even the smallest sin, even the thoughts I had toward others—of dislike, anger, hate, or frustration—seemed so big. To see my grievous sins was absolutely terrible.

Jesus showed me the state of my soul, which was putrid. He revealed that my sins not only hurt other people but even led them into sin, such as when they imitated me or responded with anger or violence. I felt so ashamed, so unworthy.

I wanted to run away but could not, and Jesus would not leave me. Worse yet, he kept me telling me he loved me and longed to forgive me.

Then the view changed, and I saw Jesus in the Garden of Gethsemane, taking into his heart the suffering and hurt from my sins and everyone else's from the beginning through the end of time. It is no wonder he sweated blood.

I saw the strokes of the whip and the crown of thorns as my sins. I saw Jesus carrying the Cross and myself sitting on top of it with my pride, making it heavier and heavier. I saw each of the nails, the thrust of the spear.

I saw Jesus hanging on the Cross just loving me, and calling out that he wanted to forgive me no matter how much I hurt him. "Through all those times," he said, "I was still there by your side loving you."

I fell to the ground crying, seeing how much throughout my life I had hurt my sweet, gentle, and wonderful Lord.

I didn't want to live. I begged him to let me die and to send me to hell because I didn't feel that I should exist anymore.

But Jesus kept calling out to me. For five hours, I cried and cried, curled up on the floor, sobbing like a baby, begging Jesus, "Let me die, let me die!"

To see His Blood running down his face as he called out to me through his suffering, "I love you, and I want to forgive you," was the deepest pain I've ever felt in my life.

Eventually with his grace, I built up the courage to ask for his forgiveness. Reaching out across a chasm of shame,

I said, "Forgive me, dear Jesus."

"I do forgive you," he answered.

At that moment, I felt a tremendous weight of sin being lifted from me. His love touched my soul in such a wonderful way that I never wanted to lose his presence again. Having him, I knew, was the most important thing in life.

I felt renewed—a different person! I couldn't stop telling Jesus that I loved him and wanted to love him forever. I knew I could never hurt him again purposefully, and I never wanted to be away from him. I fell in love with Jesus that day, and I totally committed my life to God.

After I asked for the Lord's forgiveness, Jesus said to me, "Go to Confession."

"Wait a minute!" I responded. "I've just been through five hours of crying my eyes out, begging you to let me die and send me to hell, while you took me through all these sins I committed, and then you said you forgave me. Now, why do I need to go to Confession?"

I thought Confession was a power trip for the priest. After you tell him what you've done wrong, he tells you off, gives you some prayers as a punishment, then you go outside, say them as quick as you can, and rush out of the church. The next time you see the priest, you avoid him.

Knowing my thoughts, Jesus said to me, "It's not that at all. You need to have the grace through the sacrament to help you through your weaknesses."

So I learned directly from the Lord he gave us Confession to help us, strengthen us, purify us, cleanse us—to bring us closer and closer to God and to heal our souls.

"It is important that you go," Jesus told me. "You must confess all your sins."

Off I went into the confessional and said, in effect, "Please, Father, forgive me, for I have sinned. I stole this little thing and told this little lie, and forgive me for anything else I've done."

I figured that covered it. I didn't want the priest to know how bad I really was.

When I came out of the confessional, Jesus said, "When you don't confess all your sins, you hold onto the pain and hurt and suffering that comes with them. If you do not confess all of your sins, it is easy for Satan to lead you into more sin because you are not only left feeling bad about yourself, but you also have that sin residing on your heart, on your very soul. It remains a weakness there, a doorway where evil can enter and lead you further away from God.

"It is also important that you continue to recognize your mistakes, and once you do, come to Confession and ask for forgiveness. Don't push them aside and say they aren't important. Understand that it is important to get rid of every sin."

I went back to Reconciliation the next day and confessed all the big sins I could remember. I was in the confessional box such a long time, crying and blubbering, that I started to feel very sorry for the priest.

Many times, I have said to Saint Stephen, Saint Matthew, and Saint Andrew, "Why me? There are so many good people who come to church because they love God, so many religious people, yet you are talking to me who has been so bad, who is so bad. I just don't understand."

They explained, "It's because God loves you, and he loves you the same as anyone else. The only difference is how much you love God. Also, by God appearing to you, someone who was so far away from him, it shows that his love is there for everyone, even the worst sinner, not just for a select few."

When Jesus forgave me from the Cross, and I accepted, I told him that whatever he asked of me, I would do, regardless. And he keeps me to that. Every time I don't want to do a request of his, he reminds me of that promise. When God came into my life, the first thing I wanted to do was quit the job I thought I would never leave to do his work, and that is exactly what Jesus asked of me.

He said, "It's going to be difficult. It's never going to be easy until the day you die. But don't give up!"

From the beginning of my ministry in 1994, I have sought the sanction and guidance of the Church. The Archbishop of Perth, Most Reverend Barry Hickey, first supported me for seventeen years. I saw him often, and he appointed a spiritual director who checked all of my writings and supervised my work.

After him, Archbishop Timothy Costelloe and his auxiliary bishop, Don Sproxton, have given me their support, which is documented in writing.

The mission Jesus gave me is to go out into the world and tell people that God loves them, and that he does not want to condemn or punish them. Since then, the Lord has sent me around the globe to be his instrument of healing, and to bring people closer to him and his Church.

The Lord has said so often that there is a day of judgment coming. No one knows when, and I do not profess to know. What Jesus says to me is to tell people to pray and receive the sacraments, turn back to God, love God, and love each other. Then when that day of judgment comes, they will be rewarded by God, not punished.

I believe that the Warning or the Mini-Judgment, which many people are concerned about and some are looking forward to, is akin to what the Lord took me through. I hope I will never have to experience it again, but I am sure that I will. By suddenly taking away those rose-colored glasses through which we see only the goodness in ourselves and think of how wonderful we are, by showing us how we have really been living and how offensive to God our sins are, he hopes we will not want to sin anymore.

"Change, pray, receive the sacraments, love each other, do not hurt each other. Live in God's love and avoid hell because if you do not, that is probably the place where you will go."

This is the message, the message he gave to me. This is the message he is giving to anyone who will listen. God is real, and he is offering everyone his love, his love forever in heaven.

Vince Sigala

I was a joyful kid. My earliest memories of childhood were beautiful. I'm not sure when all that changed for me. I only remember that my home was happy, and then it wasn't. I can recall running to my father and yelling "Daddy!" with glee when he came home from work, and how proud my dad looked when I caught my first fish. My father meant more to me than anything or anyone. He was my hero.

My memories jump from that wellspring of goodness to seeing my father brought home by the police, to seeing him cursing, screaming, and beating my mom with a belt, to feeling him grip me to his chest with a butcher knife to my throat, threatening to kill me if mom didn't give him money for another heroin fix, to seeing my hero in prison for burglary.

I remember the concrete floor and the brick walls as I ran down that hallway to hug my daddy. But now he was dressed in an orange jump suit. I don't remember seeing my father very much after that. Mom divorced him while he was in prison because she feared if she did so when he was out, he would kill her.

My mom, brother, and I were then on our own. Mom was often gone from our home in Salinas, California, working two jobs to pay the bills, and I only heard from Dad around Christmastime and birthdays. I remember one Christmas Eve, in particular, when Dad called to say he was coming over with a big surprise for my younger brother and me.

Throughout Christmas eve night, I was overwhelmed with anticipation and sheer joy, and every second of Christmas day, I asked, "Mom, when is Dad going to be here?"

But Christmas day came and went. I vividly recall lying at the foot of the front door, crying uncontrollably, while my mom tried to comfort me. All I could say was, "I want my dad. I just want to see my dad."

He never came. Didn't even call.

By the time I started fourth grade, babysitters, whom my mom knew and trusted, had molested me three times. I felt dirty and different, depressed and filled with disgust, but tried to hide my feelings, even from myself.

Exactly one year later to the day, on Christmas morning in 1975, when I was in second grade, I had my first mystical experience. My mother took my brother and me to church. After Mass, we walked out the front doors of Saint Mary of the Nativity Church, where Fr. Richard was greeting parishioners. Standing near Father, I looked up and saw the glory of God shining behind him. The light was pure, like crystal, but imbued with color and regenerating from within itself—alive and exceedingly beautiful.

In the fourth grade, Mom moved me from a public school to a Catholic one. I was wild, a real source of penance to the nuns, and a reason for all the teachers to look forward to the weekend. Initially, I hated the transfer, but it turned out to be one of the best decisions my mom ever made.

From the moment I entered Catholic school, I knew, by no will of my own, that I would marry a girl who went to the same school, had the same number of letters in her first name as in mine, and that my first born would be a son. I spent a lot of time in class trying to figure out who it might be. This was a big deal. Few girls had the right number of letters, and if they did, I didn't find them attractive. Oddly, I simply understood that this had to happen, and the incongruence of this future reality ate at me. I just couldn't figure it out.

In the sixth grade, I began attending a youth group called Son Beams, whose director, Cheryl Ward, took us teens under her wing, as did the woman who assisted her, Faye. I went to this group at Cheryl's house for the snacks and the girls, but as I continued showing up, something started to tug on my heart.

In one of our meetings, we wrote a letter to Jesus, and that "something" revealed itself to me as Someone. For the first time in seven years, I met Someone with whom I could share freely about my dad, Someone who I sensed would not only listen and understand, but who really cared.

When I was in eighth grade, at one of our last meetings, the lower grades were invited to Cheryl's for an open house of sorts so the graduating kids could invite them to the youth group. I noticed a fourth grade girl sitting on the arm of a chair.

"Hi, my name is Vince."

"Hi, I'm Heather."

I stood there staring at her big, beautiful green eyes, then blurted out, "Wow, you're really pretty. If you were older, I would ask you out."

I had unwittingly introduced myself to my future wife! Same school, same number of letters as V-i-n-c-e-n-t, and our first born would be a nine-pound, ten-ounce baby boy named Christian. It never occurred to me that the girl I had spent so much time trying to find would be four grades below me—God's sense of humor.

I eventually attended a different youth group, but I never got as much out of it as I did from Cheryl's. I wasn't receiving holy corrections there and my relationship with God was not a priority. I was more a nuisance than anything else.

I eventually found myself with an insignificant dilemma, although it seemed gargantuan to me. I liked two girls who liked me and I wasn't sure which one to ask out, so I called Cheryl.

"Well, God could answer that question better than me," she told me. "Why don't you pray about it and ask the Lord for an answer, and then open your Bible and start reading?"

I said, "OK," hung up and did what she said. No answer. So, I called her back. "Nothing happened, and I did exactly what you said."

Cheryl directed me to repeat the process. "This time pray with your heart. Really talk to him. Believe you will receive an answer."

So again, I prayed, this time hard, and opened the Bible. From the first words, God spoke to me clearly and directly. His Word sliced into me and had nothing to do with my question.

The Scripture passage I opened to was Isaiah 48: "Hear this, O house of Jacob called by the name Israel, sprung from the stock of Judah, you who swear by the name of the Lord and invoke the God of Israel without sincerity, without justice."

I sensed God was speaking directly about my insincerity towards him, and he convicted my heart to its core.

By holding up a mirror, God opened my eyes. Then came another message in verse 6, which struck my heart, although I didn't understand its meaning:

> From now on I announce new things to you, hidden events you never knew. Now, not from of old, they are created, before time you did not hear of them, so that you cannot claim, 'I have known them.' You never heard, you never knew, they never reached your ears beforehand.

Years later, this is exactly what God did. He was planning to reveal to me visions of future events concerning the world and the Church. But that verse would have to wait. Meanwhile, in verse 20, came the calling: "With shouts of joy declare this, announce it; make it known to the ends of the earth, say: The Lord has redeemed his servant Jacob."

I believed the Lord was commanding my spirit to proclaim redemption, specifically my own, and to preach the Gospel in all Truth without compromise, but I felt somewhat fearful because it sounded like God was angry with me, so I called Cheryl and she quickly calmed my spirit.

"Well Vincent, it sounds to me like Someone's talkin' to ya. You want my advice? I'd listen to what He's sayin'."

The next day at school, Bible in hand, I told all my friends to stop sinning and turn to God. "God is real!" and "He loves you." They didn't know what to make of it. I had gone from being one of the cool guys to preaching repentance. I barely knew what to make of it. My best friends began avoiding me. I could be overly aggressive, and they were paying Christianity lip-service, like I had done.

I began to give talks at the youth group retreats and felt a holy desire to share God's love with others, especially with one of the girls. We prayed together, talked for hours about Jesus, and became a couple at the tender age of thirteen.

I loved her, but she also became an idol. At the end of the eighth grade, she broke up with me. She learned that being a true Christian came with persecution and began to distance herself and then broke away, not only from me, but from God. I watched in despair as she returned to the comfort of being accepted by those who knew nothing of God and sought the things of the world to make them happy.

I felt alone again and lacked spiritual direction. The youth leaders tried but couldn't understand me. Neither could I.

This was so much more than splitting up. The pain that crashed down upon me was tenfold what I had experienced with my father. I desperately wanted her salvation and was in absolute anguish. The only words that made any sense to me were the Lord's, "My soul is sorrowful, even unto death."

Still seeking spiritual direction, I went to a priest in my hometown, but in one of our private meetings, he put his hand on my leg. Before this, he had bought me gifts. Preceding his transfer to another parish, he had called my mother, asking for her permission to take me to a mountain cabin, and she forcefully hung up on him. When he touched my leg, I knew exactly what was happening. I had already been there before and so I ran. I ran from the youth group, from the pain, from everything and everyone.

I entered an all-male Catholic school and spent most of my free time alone with my Bible, trying hard to understand why a God who supposedly loved me so much would allow me to experience such pain. The little contact I did have with others usually happened in a negative way, since I quickly became a target of older bullies. But I wasn't going to be pushed around, so their taunts often led to physical confrontations. It didn't take long for them to learn not to mess with me.

Playing football freshman year provided my only bright spot, because it allowed me to channel my anger, stay out of trouble, and receive praise. Had my coaches known the rage from which my aggression came they would have discouraged it. But violence was a part of the game. I intended to punish and hurt the opponent. This didn't bother me in the least.

By the end of the year, my mother received a letter from the school, saying that I would not be allowed to return due to numerous fights. As a result, I went back into the public school and into a rapid descent toward a living hell.

I entered my sophomore year with the mentality that I could count on no one but myself. My dad didn't care about me. Those I trusted had violated me. A priest had failed me.

Did God, who had showed me his love, only do so to allow me to experience even more pain? Hurt became anger. Anger matured into hate. And hate devolved into blind rage.

On the second day of my sophomore year of high school, I got in a fight during lunch hour, beginning of a long string of violent altercations. My target was a boy who had taunted me the previous summer, calling my mother names and talking "big" behind my back, but never confronting me head on.

I cornered him in a field and with my friends egging me on, and his friends doing the same to him, I approached him. He told me he didn't want to fight. I didn't care. I unleashed years of fury on this poor kid. I hit him in the face so many times that I broke my hand as he was begging me to stop.

The next thing I remember was holding him by the back of his hair and smashing his face into the gravel track, then standing over him and repeatedly kicking him as hard as I could in the head and face with my heavy Colorado boots.

Had my friends not pulled me off him, I don't know that I would have stopped. I will never forget the boy I saw when his friends helped him to his feet. His face no longer resembled a face. All I could see was blood and torn flesh. That image, like an ugly scar, is burned into my memory.

The next eight years of my life blurred into an unholy mix of heavy metal music, violence, drunkenness, drug use, and unbridled sex. I swallowed the big lie that Vince was no longer a victim of the world but in control over it. The reality was, the moment I decided to take control was the moment I completely lost it. I could not get through the day without getting high on marijuana, which numbed me from everything I wanted to forget, and led to hard drugs like cocaine.

Through my frequent fornication, I began to judge women based on their appearance and how good they were in bed. I woke up next to women whose names I didn't even know.

But there was one girl who was different. She had lived around the corner from me in Salinas, but I only got to know her better through a mutual friend when I was twenty-one.

We started to do most everything together and soon were best friends. After three years, I finally mustered the nerve to kiss her. My feelings for her were genuine. We started dating, and when her parents decided to relocate to Lodi, they gave her the choice to leave behind everything she knew and have college paid for, or, to remain and be on her own. She decided to stay and moved in with me.

When I was twenty-four and playing lead guitar in a band with a promising future, she announced that she was pregnant. She was nineteen.

Her name was spelled H-e-a-t-h-e-r.

In an instant, that distant memory came rushing back—the same number of letters, the same school! And we soon learned that the child in her womb was boy. I told myself that my son would never know ugliness in his father, like I had, so I quit the band, got a good paying job, and married her.

We bought our first home, and things seemed to be going well. Though we fought often, we made our relationship work for our son, Christian. We were making good money, so our relationship found strength in materialism. I had gotten my contractor's license and was doing specialty flooring in the Monterey Bay area for high-end clientele: Clint Eastwood's properties, The Monterey Bay Aquarium, etc.

My work ethic and job integrity stemmed from my mom's example of hard work when I was young. Our family's little world revolved around three things: work, money, and the baby. We were not living our Catholic faith, not even close.

After five years our life together began to sink. The spark was gone and we had grown apart. Nothing made us happy. I fell into a deep depression, and one night, I pondered taking my own life. I was sitting on our bed with a loaded gun in my hand as my wife cooked dinner and my nine-year-old son played in the living room.

I reviewed my life: I had used numerous drugs and downed gallons of alcohol; I had hurt many people in fights; I had slept with countless women.

And here I was, a husband and father, trying to do things right, and more miserable than when I was doing everything wrong. True joy, I thought, must be a myth.

The only thing stopping me from putting the gun into my mouth and pulling the trigger was the faint sound of my son's voice in the other room.

Heather wasn't religious, but in a last-ditch effort to save our marriage and save me from myself, she handed me a book that night called **The Purpose Driven Life** by Rick Warren. From the first page, I knew Who was speaking to me. I knew what was missing. The only real joy I had ever felt had never come from the world.

The next day I called up Cheryl, whom I hadn't spoken to in years. She told me the place to begin was Confession and recommended I see a particular priest. "Fr. Jim Nisbet is a world-renowned Scripture scholar with great wisdom. Listen to him." Then she confided, "I've been praying and waiting for this phone call for a long time."

Determined to follow her advice, I went to see the priest. Sporting jeans with holes in the knees, dirty sneakers, and a tank top, I walked into his office.

"What can I do for you?" he asked.

"I need to do a Confession. I have a calling."

In the most intellectual voice I have ever heard, he asked with a smirk, "Really. What kind of calling?"

"A calling to preach the Word of God."

He smiled, looked at me like I was a nut, and holding in laughter, agreed and proceeded to hear my confession.

At Cheryl's suggestion, I asked if it would be okay to meet on a regular basis. He almost never took on spiritual direction in this manner, but by the grace of God, agreed.

That year, I met with him regularly and immersed myself in prayer, particularly the Rosary, the Scriptures, and the daily reception of the Eucharist. With great anticipation and an all-consuming need to receive the Body and Blood of Christ, I practically ran into church for Mass each day.

Fr. Nisbet encouraged me to forgive all those in my past who had hurt me, even the babysitters who had molested me, to tell them in person or over the phone that I forgave them. I did try to reach them, but to no avail.

I was, however, able to reach my father. When I called him, I got right to the point. "Dad, I want to let you know that I forgive you for everything you did to me and to our family."

My father immediately broke down crying and said, "Thank you."

A great weight was lifted from both of us that night, not to say that it was easy. It was the hardest phone call I have ever made.

In early 2003 I began experiencing unusual phenomena, not unknown in the Church, but definitely unknown to me. I began receiving private revelations via visions and locutions, without knowing what these were called.

I thought the only people who ever experienced stuff like this were in the Bible. And why in the world would such things happen to someone like me, who had offended the Lord in so many ways? I was merely trying to come back to the Church.

The first vision happened when I was sitting on our living-room couch one evening. Suddenly...

I found myself in the midst of a large crowd of people. They were yelling loudly and there was angry pushing and shoving, but a few people were weeping, mostly women. I could not understand the language they were speaking and felt both surprised and disconcerted, for no other reason than I found myself there in the blink of an eye by no will of my own. The people were dressed in what appeared to be Middle-Eastern attire, and the road on which we stood was paved by hand in cobblestone.

No sooner was I able to orient myself when I caught glimpses of a certain man through the crowd. All attention was on him, as he slowly made his way toward me from my right. The pushing, shoving, and yelling was increasing to a violent intensity. I could feel my body being pushed back and forth, and I struggled to maintain my balance.

The man came so close as to pass in front of me, just three people away. I could make out his hair, which was somewhat long and completely soaked in what looked to be his own blood. The one-piece white garment he wore was filthy and also stained with blood in places. I could see clearly his crown of thorns, and the front and left side of his head where the thorns were deeply embedded into his scalp; it was the swelling of these wounds that drew most of my attention. They were large and purple, filled with blood underneath the skin, disfiguring his brow.

A large, heavy beam of wood lay across the back of his shoulders and neck. His arms were tied to it at the elbows, and his forearms were hanging towards the ground. He was stumbling, barely able to take his next step.

As a spectator, I did not know that this man was the Lord until after the vision ended. Yet I distinctly remember thinking that I must help him—that I had to do something to help him.

When I took a step forward to reach him through the few people in front of me, another man on my right pushed me out of the way with great force. I stumbled to my left, and as I regained my balance, the man walked up to the Lord at arm's length and threw a large rock, about the size of a brick, as hard as he could. It crashed into the side of Jesus' head with a brutal force.

The sound of the impact was gruesome and mixed with a gush of air that released from his mouth, and a low, gasping moan. As he fell away from me to the ground under force of the blow, he tried to brace himself from the fall, but couldn't because his arms were tied to the wood. When he landed, his arms crumpled under the weight of his body and the wood, with the front his face taking the brunt of the fall onto the stone path.

He lay there, rocking from side to side in obvious and unbelievable pain. People then began to kick him in the stomach, head, and legs.

The vision ended as quickly as it began. It was so real! I was there, no differently than I am here on earth right now. What an enormous price the Lord paid for my sins! Until then, I had never truly understood the sheer brutality of the Passion of our Lord, and I shuddered with the realization of how he had felt every strike, every kick, every punch I had ever inflicted on a fellow human being.

Heather came into the room and saw my tears. She asked me what was wrong, and I collapsed to my knees in front of her, wrapping my arms around her hips.

Crying profusely, all I could manage to say was, "He loves us so much, Heather, he loves us so much."

My second vision came around a week later and was just as real as the first. Whether I wanted it or not, or understood it or not, the Lord began to do exactly what he said he would when he first spoke to me in Isaiah 48:

> From now on I announce new things to you, hidden events you never knew. Now, not from of old, they are created, before time you did not hear of them, so that you cannot claim, 'I have known them.' You never heard, you never knew, they never reached your ears beforehand.

One morning I left the house to run errands, and suddenly...

> I saw the sky opening up and Jesus coming on the clouds of heaven. It was as if the air itself opened to reveal the unseen. The Lord was enormous, and I was made to know that everyone, no matter where they were on Earth, would see this. His hands, which still bore the wounds from the nails, were down by his waist, turned outward, as though presenting himself, and he was surrounded in great power and glory.
>
> White clouds moved by with tremendous speed and power, inflamed with a reddish orange fire. White lights, small and bright, which I understood to be angels, darted to and fro around him.

This experience would seem to bring with it at least some trepidation. But I had no fear. Instead I was instilled with a joyous sense of victory, something I have never felt before or since. My triumphant exuberance was so strong I wanted to leave everything and run to the Lord as fast as my legs could take me.

This feeling remained long after the vision ended.

I didn't tell anyone about the vision and I still knew nothing of mysticism. I had no idea such things still happened. To be honest, part of me grew concerned. Although not to the point of panic, I wondered if I was losing it. Everything was moving so fast; I received one vision and barely had enough time to realize what happened before the next.

During this period, I would stay up very late reading the Scriptures and talking to Jesus during the day. Even though my sleep habits had changed, I never woke up tired, and my prayer life didn't interfere with my work in any way.

My morning routine was to wake up, make some coffee, pray the Rosary or read Scripture, get ready, drop off my son at school, and head to morning Mass before work.

Within several days of the vision of Jesus in the heavens, my small fear of being crazy was replaced with a holy fear of God. In April 2003 I woke up at 4:00 am and was compelled to get up and pray. I walked down the hallway of my house, and as I approached the kitchen, I was immediately *taken away*. All I know is that *the I*, whom I know to *be me*, with all of his hopes, fears, feelings, sights, smells, and touch, was no longer in my hallway.

A great flash of blinding white light temporarily impaired my vision, and as my eyes adjusted, I could see before me, a round lake of water, bearing little resemblance to any on earth. It looked more like a thin slice of crystal, smooth as glass, with light emanating from beneath its surface.

In the center of the lake there stood a tree-like fountain, which poured forth multi-colored lights, like streams of water.

Both the ground around the lake and the sky above were pure light. Across the lake, I could see human figures dressed in white robes, too bright to make out in detail, due to the immense brilliance of a great white light to the right of me in my peripheral vision.

This glorious light, like crystal, yet alive, was God himself. As I focused on the figures conversing amongst themselves, suddenly appearing in front of them was the Lord, Jesus Christ. I could clearly see his face, his beard, his hair, and the outline of his ankle-length robe, which glowed with brilliance. Tall and strong with sharp features and white hair, like pristine snow, he looked like a king.

Facing toward my right, Jesus began levitating, slowly and purposefully, toward the brilliant light which was the Father. Then with his right hand extended forward, and the back of his right shoulder facing me, he reached into the light, whose brightness obscured my view of his extended arm. When he brought his hand out, he was holding the scroll with seven seals from the Book of Revelation. The scroll appeared off-white with a hint of bronze, and was about three feet long. Its seals were thick, round, and the color of dark-red blood.

The Lord turned to face me and looked directly at me. My entire being immediately seized with a tremendous fear of God. Unable to move or breathe, I felt petrified, as though I were about to die. His pupils were flames of fire that pierced through the center of my soul. Nothing was hidden from his gaze. All that I had ever done in my life lay absolutely bare before him...

In a flash, Our Lord began to show me, interiorly, my past sins and their consequences. I had no control over what was happening to me. I saw every transgression that I had knowingly and unknowingly committed. What I had thought were little things, like yelling at my brother or my mom, weren't little at all; and my sins of omission, actions I should have taken but didn't—which I didn't know were sins at all—struck my heart with tremendous regret and sorrow.

Nine years of my life passed in a blur, and I didn't realize how far I had fallen into darkness until I was shown its true ugliness. The more that I saw, the more it got worse.

Everything had been about me and my pleasure. The world had been my playground. Whatever I wanted I went and got; whatever I couldn't easily get, I went somewhere else to find.

Christ, the King and Lord of All, was exposing my deceit and anger, my physical and emotional violence, my lust and abuse, my arrogance and slander, my materialism and greed, my idol worship and vanity, my alcohol and drug use, my partying and rock music: all the things I held in higher esteem than God. Most of my life had been wasted pleasing myself and impressing others, but not Him.

Particularly devastating was the destructiveness that my actions had on other people. I had led many of God's children into sin.

One event in particular stood out like a glaring nightmare. After having sex with a girl, I introduced her to cocaine, and then we lost contact. Three years later, I saw her again. She was hardly recognizable. Addicted to crack, she appeared old, crinkled, gaunt, and weary. Jesus showed me how she allowed herself be used sexually and physically, over and over. My inordinate desires had destroyed her life.

The Lord revealed how Satan had used my twisted view of sexuality, caused by the three molestations in my life, to turn me into an instrument of death. The abuse predisposed me to lust, rather than love. Out of my lust came fornication, and my fornication led to two young women having abortions, which then made me partially guilty of murder.

I was shown how when I was a little kid, around five years old, someone gave my older sister a playboy magazine, and I felt so upset and hurt that I ran into another room and started crying. Later in life, when I used pornography, I saw nothing wrong with it at all.

What horrified me and left me shaking the most was seeing the nature of sin itself. It does nothing but destroy and is infinitely worse than poison. Poison can kill the body, which is temporal, but sin can kill the soul, which is eternal.

Jesus revealed to me that each individual sin is significant, large or small. A little lie is serious because the Lord looks at our hearts. A lie may seem small, but the deceit within us can be huge. It is the same with slander (casting another in a negative light) because thinking it can look the same in God's eyes as speaking it; He sees the seed of judgment in our hearts. The spoken slander is simply an expression of it.

Lust is the same. Jesus said in Matthew 5: 27-28, "You have heard that it was said, 'You shall not commit adultery.' But I say to you, everyone who looks at a woman with lust has already committed adultery with her in his heart." He meant exactly what he said.

God revealed how sin spreads like a malignant cancer. Just the simple act of treating one person negatively initiates a spider-web effect. If I yell at someone in the morning and put them in a bad mood, they take that with them into their day and spread it easily to others, who in turn, bring the anger home with them, and take it out on their loved ones, who bother their neighbors, and so on. Like the many branches of an infinite, insidious tree, it expands from one small sprout. Every single sin multiplies this way, even those we think are hidden, affecting both the physical and the spiritual realms, and can travel across *generations*, sometimes *continents*.

Sin unveiled is a gruesome thing.

What happened next shocked me to my core. I was standing before Jesus, with no memory of how I had come back to the Church two years earlier and repented. The Lord of heaven and earth was hiding this from my awareness because he was about to let me fully experience what would have happened to me had I died in my sins.

Jesus gave me my personal judgment. I saw my sentence within his eyes. The verdict was hell for all eternity. I was frozen, speechless, in an overwhelming, silent terror. I knew I deserved it, and there was absolutely nothing I could do to stop it. The experience was frightful beyond sheer horror.

I couldn't argue back. I couldn't talk my way out of anything. I fell silent before the divine truth that justice demands. I was undergoing my personal judgment in miniature, and by the life I had lived, I had freely chosen my sentence: an eternal "fiery furnace, where there will be wailing and grinding of teeth."

Human language cannot convey the regret that seized me.

As Jesus took the scroll from the Father, I was also made to understand that this judgment, unique to each individual, is coming *upon the world.* Every person on the face of the earth will experience their personal judgment, either while alive or at death, and every single sin will have to be accounted for.

What made the experience so scary, and what makes me so concerned for the world, is that at death there is no way to alter one's sentence. There is no way to go back and change things, to correct the wrongs. It is absolute. In my vision, the door to heaven had been locked with an iron deadbolt, and my fate was to be sealed forever.

My experience in the heavenly realm stopped as quickly as it began, and I found myself back at the end of my hallway. There was a distant echo of holy chanting in the air, and my body was trembling uncontrollably from head to toe. As the day went on, I prayed harder than I ever had, begging God for mercy, begging him to give the world more time, as we are not ready for this. For the sake of poor sinners, for humanity, for the sake of his Holy Name, I begged him to have mercy!

It took close to seven months for me to come to the full realization of what had happened that morning in the hallway. I was not only shown my sin for what it truly was, but what everyone will experience during what I later learned is called the Warning.

To recollect it even now brings tears to my eyes and an overwhelming sadness for the world, simply because I know what awaits each person if he or she doesn't repent and turn back to God. There will be many who will not survive this. Their bodies will physically not be able to withstand an encounter with their sin, as seen within the Holiness of the Living God. Simply put, they will die of sheer fright at the sight of their own sin. That is how I understood this. Some will drop dead, some will convert, and others will completely reject God and become possessed by Satan.

A day or so later, two women I didn't know approached me; they stopped me in the parking lot after morning Mass, as I was walking to my truck, and offered me a pamphlet.

"We feel like we're supposed to give this to you."

I inquired a little, and they said it was information about a pilgrimage. I'd heard of pilgrimages before, but they were talking about a place I had never heard of and could not even pronounce: Medjugorje in Bosnia-Herzegovina.

I took the pamphlet to be polite. The last thing on my mind was a Marian pilgrimage. My marriage was a mess, I was going through radical changes, and while I did pray the Rosary, I would never have considered myself close to Mary. A relationship with the Mother of God was foreign to me.

A week or so later, I took a break during work. Outside the house I was working on, I said a little prayer, and reflected on the graces I'd been receiving. I used to turn on my truck radio and listen to preachers or Christian music. On this day I heard a man preaching. Naive to how Catholics are looked down upon by so many Protestants, I thought we all got along.

He was teaching about the Rapture and End Times from the Book of Revelation. I didn't know the Catholic Church's views on these things. (I have since learned that there is no such thing as a pre-tribulation rapture—a moment when all the good people will be taken away, or raptured, and all the wicked will be left behind to suffer the final tribulation. The pre-tribulation rapture is not in the Bible.)

Near the end of his sermon, he added sarcastically, "Boy, the Catholics will be surprised when it happens." This was followed by laughter and applause.

Something was very wrong because I knew so many good Catholics like Cheryl, Faye, Fr. Nisbet, and all the nuns who taught me. So if anyone was supposed to be raptured, it was them. This guy was a good preacher, and I enjoyed him, but I couldn't understand. I immediately bowed my head, praying, "Lord, please give me understanding of your Word."

When I looked up, my gaze fixed upon a tree across the street while the preacher's voice began to lower until it was gone. Simultaneously I began to feel a current, similar to a growing wind, but spiritual in nature. It grew, swirling around to envelope me, and I found it harder and harder to breath.

Then it stopped. Air was no longer there, as if I no longer needed it to live. I found myself frozen and unable to move, staring at God's Glory appearing before me. This was different than a vision. His manifestation of Glory was physically in front of me. I could still make out the tree and the scene across the street through it…

The Glory of God was like crystal, yet living, with every color of the rainbow slowly emanating long, luminous, translucent shards outward from within it. It exuded a powerful heat, which could consume all things in any moment, but stayed controlled and purposefully didn't overwhelm me; and it possessed a quality of purity not of this world. Within the vision of Glory, scenes of moving images, sharp and in full color, began passing before my eyes in slow motion: The Lord was showing me future events concerning a great tribulation in the world, which shook the depths of my soul.

Transfixed, I saw a world war in the future, a nuclear exchange between nations, great social unrest, worldwide chaos, people possessed by Satan, future chastisements: mankind, by its own actions, bringing itself to the very point of extinction.

I saw the infiltration of the Church by those in league with Lucifer, a massive persecution of the Church, from within and without, with priests being murdered, churches sacked and burned, and the Holy Eucharist trampled and profaned by soldiers with faces of death.

The earth was made desolate, and destruction reigned everywhere. It appeared as if all the demons of hell had been unleashed upon Earth while man unleashed the most terrible weapons upon himself.

When this vision stopped, I raced to my truck, turned off the radio, grabbed my Bible, and opened to the Book of Daniel.

I somehow knew that what I had been shown was written there. After I read just a few scattered verses in Chapters 7 through 12, strands of luminous golden wheat woven together in three ropes came up through the left-hand side of my Bible and buried themselves into the right. The golden light of the ropes shone brighter and brighter, accompanied by a sound like the strong hum of an electric current. As the three ropes bore down into the pages with tremendous force, the sound and the light came to a crescendo, and two words came into my mind: "totally binding."

That is to say, I knew the vision must happen, that there is no way around it, and no amount of prayer can stop it. It is written. It is part of God's plan of purification, decreed by him through his holy prophets, and according to his will.

The Lord gave me another vision in which I believe I was shown a divine act of God through which the truly faithful were protected from a certain and devastating chastisement of divine justice:

I was suddenly standing in the back of a church. Behind me were two, solidly heavy, large wooden doors. There was no way through this entrance from the outside and no way out from the inside. I was made to know that the doors had been locked by God Himself.

Outside of the doors, there was great confusion, chaos, horror, fear, and death. As I looked toward the altar, a priest was elevating the Sacred Host, and people were kneeling in the pews and in the aisles, some with their heads touching the ground. Not a sound came from any of them, only great reverence and silence. When the Host had reached its highest elevation, crystal clear water, somewhat thick and with light emanating from within it, flowed out from the Sacred Host and into the air. This water was alive, and it slowly washed over everyone there.

I was then transported at lightning speed to another church somewhere else in the world, where all the above happened again, only faster. I sensed that this Mass was being held around the world at the same time. The same scene was shown to me repeatedly, only faster each time it happened. I understood the water from the Host to be some type of divine protection from what was happening outside of the sanctuaries.

Later, God would show me the victory of his Holy Church and his people in the world, preserved and renewed by the Spirit of Almighty God through the intercession of the Blessed Mother, after all that was unholy had been removed.

As I stood outside on a dirt path, I saw a group of about fifty to a hundred people walking in the same direction away from me, as if going somewhere. I sensed their great reverence for the Church and the Sacraments. God was their first love, far and above all else, and their love for one another was without barriers. They were smiling and laughing as they talked and interacted with one another. The adults appeared to be in their late twenties to early thirties, and were accompanied by a few children running around, just being kids.

The sky was extremely clear without any pollution, the clearest I had ever seen. Various plants were scattered to my far left and right, and the path disappeared into distant rolling hills covered in grass. All of creation, the sky and the land, was renewed with divine life. The peace of God, which lies beyond all human understanding and fulfills human longing, had been poured out upon Earth.

I was seeing a future world where there is no sickness or pain, where life is much simpler and people live much longer than they do now. I noticed peoples' skin radiated in a way foreign to what we know now. Everyone looked beautiful, healthier, and more luminous because of God's presence within them. There was no sign of makeup, hair spray, or revealing clothes. People walked around comfortably in loosely fitting pants and tunics, which were light in color, different from any styles of today. Nothing looked modern, and yet everything looked new.

I distinctly remember one man at the tail end of the group. He turned to look back at me and smiled warmly, as though inviting me to hurry up and join them. He had a beard and semi-long hair. He resembled Jesus, but in the vision, I was not made to know who he was.

Only when the vision ended did I realize this man was Jesus, shepherding his people into a new age of peace. Overwhelmed by these revelations, which were bringing me to my knees, I called Cheryl and Faye, and they encouraged me to share them with Fr. Nisbet.

"Tell him everything," they said, pushing me through my hesitation to speak, for fear of the priest's response. "He's your spiritual director, after all."

He was a little intimidating for no other reason than his great gift of wisdom. He was an encyclopedia who seemed to know everything about everything. I finally did tell Father about the visions, although I did not go into much detail at first, perhaps because I was still in a semi-state of shock.

I remember sobbing, "It's going to be a slaughter," unable to understand why all this had to be. In his familiarity with uncommon mystical gifts, Father recognized the words and visions as prophetic revelations from God. I still had no idea that I was prophesying. I was confused, overwhelmed and deeply sad, and wept every time I told him about these things.

Father's reaction was the complete opposite, nothing less than uncharacteristic outbursts of sheer joy.

"Make sure you land on the foot of faith," Father Nisbet said. "Realizing the glory to which you have been called will help you deal with the burden that comes with it."

"But, Father. Couldn't God find someone else?"

Out of curiosity I asked him what he was learning from all this. He looked at me and smiled, saying, "I'm learning that God chooses whom he will."

Soon I would receive a difficult test of faith and trust. I had been honest with Fr. Nisbet, and now I had to be honest with my family, so I shared with them what was happening to me. My wife, my friends, my brother, and his family quickly abandoned me. Even my in-laws thought I had taken a crazy pill. Only my mom, Cheryl, Faye, and Fr. Nisbet believed me.

At one point, my wife walked up to me as I was studying the Scriptures and said, "Vince, you're changing, and I don't know if I can live like this."

Holding back tears, I responded, "Heather, no matter what happens, I will always love you."

She turned and silently walked away.

A few years passed, and in 2005 our family, still intact by the grace of God, moved to another town. Now I was far away from my spiritual director and missed our meetings tremendously. I went to see my new pastor to share with him what had been happening, at the suggestion of Fr. Nisbet, with the caveat, "Don't be surprised if he thinks you're cuckoo."

He won't think I'm crazy, I thought. *He's a priest. He'll understand.*

I should have heeded his warning. Within minutes of our first meeting, I could sense the he was struggling to believe me. Passiveness is not one of my stronger traits. Once I get going, I find it hard to stop my tongue, so I persisted. Finally, I think out of sheer frustration with me, he told me the saints didn't do this kind of stuff, and referring to Proverbs, said, "Every dog will return to its own vomit." Then he excused himself so as not to waste any more of his time.

He is actually a humble, obedient priest. He did not intend to hurt me. I prayed about this, saying, "Jesus, he won't listen.

He doesn't understand. I thought it was your will that I share this, and he just won't listen!"

Jesus responded in a locution by asking me, "Why are you so impatient with my brother? Oh, my child, how often, how many times in your life have I spoken to you, and you haven't listened? Have I ever been impatient with you?"

Humbled by the Lord's words and by my selfishness and pride, I began to pray every day for this priest. Shortly after that first meeting, I was walking to my car after attending a weekday Mass and Rosary, and was approached by a woman I didn't know, again in the parking lot of a church.

"Sir!" she yelled. When I turned, she was hurrying over to me. "I'm sorry to bother you, but I really felt I should give this to you. It's information about a pilgrimage to Medjugorje."

This time, I paid close attention. She explained how she believed that Our Lady was appearing there. I took a pamphlet and mentioned it to Heather, but the thought of flying halfway around the world seemed like a far-fetched dream.

Around that time, the Blessed Mother was becoming more real to me: a true and tangible mother, not just a distant and powerful figure attached to my rosary beads. Feeling terribly alone in the world, my marriage all but over, my flooring business almost nonexistent after starting over from scratch, and finding nowhere else to turn for help, I pleaded for guidance from Mary.

Returning to the church, I knelt in an alcove before a large statue of Our Lady of Fatima, and just cried. I asked her to please help me understand all this stuff that was happening to me and what I was supposed to do with all of it—and to save my marriage. When I eventually looked up at her statue, a soft white light with smaller but brighter lights within it was raining down upon her.

Through a locution, the Blessed Mother said, "Come to my place." I knew she meant Medjugorje.

I decided to go. When the day of departure came, Heather helped to get me through the airport. I was like a kid who was completely lost and had no idea what I was doing, and to say that I was nervous would be an understatement. I didn't know my way around airports at all, and I was terrified of flying.

As I sat in a window seat, waiting for the plane to take off, I wanted to jump out. *This is a mistake,* I thought to myself. *I shouldn't have done this.*

When the engines kicked in and asphalt began to speed by, all I could think was, *What in the world are you doing? This is crazy. You're doing this for no other reason than because you heard a voice? Oh boy, this is really bad.*

During the flights to Bosnia-Herzegovina, I didn't sleep a wink. When I arrived with my pilgrimage group, I was just happy to be on the ground. Our tour guide, Matilda, an aunt of the visionary Mirjana, gave us a brief summary of Medjugorje and how the apparitions there began.

This was somewhat interesting, but I had already read a book on Medjugorje before I left and knew most of the story. I noticed that now that I was finally in Mary's Place, a spirit of peace came over me which I had never felt in the United States, and my doubts that our Blessed Mother had personally invited me vanished.

It was there my mystical experiences began to tie together. I went there searching for Mary, for answers, for peace, and I found all three. In Medjugorje, the Holy Spirit began to teach me the magnitude of all of Our Lady's messages to the Church and the world. Within them, heaven's plan is being revealed.

What I had been shown regarding imminent future events corresponded to past messages from apparitions of Our Lady, which I knew nothing about. The Spirit planted in me a seed of curiosity which led me to learn of her apparitions in La Salette, France; Fatima, Portugal; Garabandal, Spain; Akita, Japan; and Kibeho, Rwanda, among others.

In late 2002, when God's revelations to me began, I had no idea about the Illumination of Conscience, or the Warning as prophesied of at Garabandal. The Holy Spirit also showed me how Our Lady's authentic apparitions were all connected, not only to each other, but also to Jesus's revelations to Saint Faustina Kowalska, the saint of Divine Mercy.

The most profound realization of my pilgrimage was that Our Lady's messages are continuing to unfold.

My fellow pilgrims around me didn't know what God had revealed to me. To sit with them and hear them occasionally inquire with each other about the Medjugorje secrets, the last of which involved chastisements, was difficult.

Many times, I would retreat to my room or climb Cross Mountain and cry to God because if they truly understood what they wanted to know so badly, they would have never wasted time inquiring. Instead, they would have just prayed.

Whenever I needed motherly comfort, I called on Mary, and her love touched me so gently that it, too, brought me to tears. I would need this same comfort in the years to come because, in time, I would receive around forty-five visions, locutions, and revelatory dreams combined.

I tried to call Heather but I couldn't get ahold of her. She wouldn't hear from me for seven more days and wondered if I was dead or alive.

I was very much alive. With each passing day, the graces intensified. I befriended an acquaintance named Loretta, who ran a Catholic bookstore back home, and she and I decided that we wanted to spend one whole day in prayer.

The next day, we separated from the group and went to Confession, Mass, prayed the Rosary on the Hill of Apparitions, and chatted with Jesus and each other all day long. We were like Catholic kids in a candy store of miracles, while the Lord presented himself to us in different ways, all day long, like a dad spoiling his kids on a field trip. No matter what we asked of Jesus, it happened almost immediately.

I wanted to ask a priest a question, and suddenly, a priest approached us, just to talk. Loretta said she was thirsty, and someone offered us a drink. We both wanted to see the miracle of the sun and suddenly, a lady cried out, "Look at the sun!"

I stared directly into the sun without difficulty and watched it spinning in the sky like a disk. A cross appeared in its center, like on a Host, and then it began to shoot out beautiful colors. On one side of this spinning disk, the light formed a red heart, which looked almost like a soft cloud, but with sharp edges, and on the other side, an exact replica in blue: symbols of the Sacred Heart of Jesus and the Immaculate Heart of Mary.

But the greatest of all the graces that day was the time we spent in adoration of the Blessed Sacrament. Head bowed, I poured out all of my silent concerns to God.

I prayed for my marriage and for my wife's conversion. I prayed to understand what the Lord was calling me to. When I looked up, I saw the Host turn the color of blood and begin to beat like a human heart. When we left the adoration chapel, I took my rosary from my pocket and noticed that all the links of its silver chain had turned gold.

When the time came to leave, our group stayed one night in Dubrovnik. I finally got through to Heather. The first thing she said to me was that I sounded different. We talked a little, and I let her know when and where to pick me up from the airport. I felt very sad that I had to leave because in Medjugorje, I felt at home. A big part of me wanted to stay there for the rest of my life. As I sat on the plane, again in a window seat, I looked down at the ground as it sped by.

This time, I had no fear of flying.

When I returned home, a second test came. In its eleventh year, my marriage was still teetering on shaky ground. Heather and I just couldn't seem to connect, and divorce had entered both our minds more than once. I began to pray fervently to Jesus about our relationship, asking him what was wrong, what I could do to fix it, and Jesus showed me how through the years I had taken my wife for granted so many times. He showed me the gift that she truly was, and how I often didn't really listen to her or see her concerns as genuine.

The next year, I dragged my wife and my eleven-year-old son to Medjugorje because I knew that getting them there was the only hope of saving my marriage. Almost refusing to go, they complained the entire journey there and throughout the first two days of our pilgrimage. But Mother Mary prevailed. She touched my wife in a profound way, showing her that it was okay to hurt, to be vulnerable, to be a little girl in her heavenly mother's heart. Mary began to bring about my wife's conversion back to Jesus, back to the Church.

When she was at the outdoor Croatian Mass, sitting on a large piece of wood on the ground, still pondering why she was there, during the Sign of Peace, a woman behind her said, "Peace be with you," in Croatian.

Heather turned and shook the woman's hand and turned back around. Something about the woman's sincere kindness prompted Heather to turn back to tell her thank you, but the woman was nowhere to be seen, as if she had never been there. To this day, Heather believes this woman might have been an angel in human form.

As the pilgrimage continued, so did the graces. I could see the Lord working on my family, and the atmosphere of daily Mass and prayer started to rub off on Heather and Christian.

One night as we were walking through a field, after getting some ice cream, my son yelled out, "Look at the light!"

Heather and I looked up where he was pointing, and sure enough, there was a light, soft and warm with a light orange color. It was very high on a mountain, not Cross Mountain and not Apparition Hill, but a high place in between them. This is significant because there is no way to climb up to that area, which is rugged with rocks and overgrown brush. The light began to float straight down the mountain, without swerving as a person would do. Two women just behind us fell to their knees and began to pray. My family stood in awe, watching the light descend to the bottom and slowly disappear.

Three days before leaving, Heather had already signed us up, with no prodding from me, to return at the same time the next year. My wife went from telling me she wanted a divorce, complaining about going to Medjugorje, and wondering why she was even there, to looking forward to returning as soon as possible.

All of this change happened to her within one week. It is Our Lady, the Queen of Peace, whom my wife and I credit with saving our marriage.

My wife then eventually made her Confirmation, became a Mass coordinator and a member of the liturgy committee, and also became a member of our church's pastoral council. She has volunteered to coordinate buses for the Walk for Life in San Francisco and has given her testimony to local parishes.

Today, any visions or messages I receive along with those from the past, I have and will submit to a certain holy priest, who is also my current pastor and an official exorcist. I do not share any of them easily or without his approval. I pray that what I have been allowed to share helps the Lord save and heal His beloved people.

Can you imagine watching your children continually run into a busy street, telling you it's not a problem, despite all your warnings? Can you imagine knowing full well that it is only a matter of time before you will literally have to watch as they get hit by car and die?

And so it is with the Father when he looks at this world. God is tender and gentle, and he loves us far beyond what we could ever imagine. That is why he is preparing to give us a merciful warning, so he can gather his children in his loving arms and keep us safe and happy forever.

One of the last visions I have received is the one I consider the most pivotal of all because of an instruction given within the vision itself, and the instruction was not just for me, but for anyone who will listen.

This indelible experience happened in early 2015, in the middle of the night:

I was asleep in bed with my wife. Suddenly, I awoke. I sat up very quickly and looked to my left. At the entrance to our bathroom, adjoined to our bedroom, was an enormous man. He was praying on both knees with his head lowered and his hands pressed together under his chin.

Our vaulted ceilings are about thirteen feet tall. Even so, the back of his head was grazing the ceiling, so the size of this creature when standing would have been at least twenty-five feet tall. His white, ankle-length garment also glimmered with gold, and a solid-gold-colored sash was wrapped around his waist. His hair was a color in between blonde and light brown, and his feet, also very large but in proportion with the rest of his body, were strapped in brownish-bronze woven sandals.

I could plainly see a cut or bruise on his upper left cheek, and while his garment was beautiful, it was soiled and discolored from what appeared to be wounds underneath the fabric. He looked extremely sad and very tired.

I was startled to say the least, not only by his presence in my room, but by the sheer size of him. I jumped out of bed and quickly reached in my night-stand drawer to grab a firearm I keep in my room for protection.

No sooner did I point the weapon in the creature's direction, when he turned his head and looked me, saying, "Please don't do that."

At these words, a great calm came over me. I lowered the weapon to my side and just stared at him. His face was gentle, as were his eyes, but he still appeared heavy-hearted.

He then said, "Tell the people to pray the Chaplet of Divine Mercy, every day, and to offer it in reparation for the sins committed by the United States."

Then the visitation stopped. In the days that followed, through contemplation and prayer, I was shown that this being is the guardian angel of the United States, and he is losing the battle for our country to Satan and his demons.

Our prayers, specifically the one he requested, strengthen not only him, but also all the angels who fight with him. He is petitioning us for help. I came to understand that we empower angels through our prayers, just as we empower demons with our sin. Our sins and indifference open the doors to the devils and their curses, but our prayers and petitions open the doors to God's strength and blessings.

We are in grave need of prayer and penance, and sacrifices for love of God that give way to waterfalls of grace. May we surrender all that we are and all that we have to Jesus before the Day of Justice arrives.

Woe to those who would take this period of mercy for granted and put off their conversions, thinking that they can wait until the last hour. To grow in holiness can only come by way of God's grace and mercy. To grow in holiness takes time. And that time for grace and mercy is now.

Rick Wendell

It's a miracle I'm alive. I grew up a thrill seeker. When life got too mundane, I'd test its limits. My friends and I had our own versions of extreme sports. We started out with rope swings over the river, and then over cliffs. We fought each other with BB guns and played toss with fireworks, which blew off one of my friend's hands. We went camping at twenty below zero and drove at speeds over a hundred.

Four of my friends died in high-speed car wrecks, but that didn't slow me down. The result: three operations on each of my wrists, five surgeries on my left knee, one on my right, two broken ankles, a separated left shoulder from jumping off a moving freight train, and a snapped collarbone from performing flying bicycle stunts—not with a decked-out mountain bike, but a Schwinn with a banana seat. My mother said she was just trying to keep me alive.

When I was sixteen, wearing my Boy Scout uniform with a merit-badge sash and driving my '69 Ford Mustang, a police officer chased me down, jumped out of his car, pointed his gun at me, and yelled, "Put your hands on the roof, kid!"

I didn't know how to drive a car except going full blast. My parents absolutely forbade me to have a motorcycle, so when I turned eighteen, I made sure to get one. It only took me a few months to spin out in a harrowing crash followed by eight hours of surgery.

After that, people began saying, "God is saving you for something special."

Nah, I thought. *I'm just lucky.*

Achievements came easy. Mom found me poring over her medical books when I was five. I sculpted, appreciated fine art, played leads in musicals, and was the captain of our high school hockey team, with the temper to go with it. I was truly a Renaissance kid in a good sense, but my personal morals flew all over the map.

At the end of my senior year in Maplewood, Minnesota, I went to five proms with four girls. When I graduated, five hundred people paid to come to my party, replete with a live band, porta-potties, and four sixteen-gallon kegs of beer.

Coming from a practicing Catholic family, it was assumed that my two brothers and I would pray before meals, bedtime, and attend Catholic schools. Being late for Mass was not an option because my mother would force us to sit in the front row. Not my idea of a thrill. Since businesses weren't open on Sundays in the 1960s, our family would have a formal meal at grandma's house after Mass every Sunday. Catholicism was a family given, but my 1970s Catholic school faith formation was dangerously thin and punctured with holes.

"God loves you," we were told. "You'll figure it out."

I spent my first year of college at home, doing independent study with the nearby University of Wisconsin because I had forty-five pounds of plaster on three broken limbs. When I recovered, I couldn't get away from home fast enough, so I escaped to Saint John's University.

I didn't witness any examples of faith among the monks on campus, and students were not required to go to Mass on Sundays, so we didn't. My immorality mushroomed because of the lack of moral guidance, and I grew disillusioned with the idea of faith. Intellectually, I could not prove that God did not exist; but he was not relevant in my life, and he or she, or whatever, certainly was not important enough for me to modify my behavior.

Although I'd been told God was all love, I never felt him and certainly did not understand him as a loving father, perhaps because I never experienced my own father's love. The only time Dad told me he loved me was on Christmas Day after downing a couple bottles of champagne. Even though I was always an honor student, was voted outstanding artist in high school, and excelled in sports, especially contact sports, Dad never came out to watch a single one of my games and couldn't find his way to offer a hug or a compliment.

Rather, he criticized me. When I was fourteen, my father hit me for the last time, perhaps because I was getting bigger, or because my smile of sheer rage immobilized him.

I swore in my heart that day I would kill him if he touched me again.

After earning a pre-med degree, I worked for a short time in a hospital emergency room to build my résumé in order to attend medical school (like my mom had).

One Saturday night after I had survived another terrible motorcycle crash, the contract doctor in the emergency room, whom I deemed very cool, sat me down and said, "Rick, you can do this job. You have the ability, but being a physician is not what I do, it's who I am. I'm not sure you would be happy."

I listened, and instead sought out the deepest snow available, which I found in Utah. Between hitting the slopes in wintertime as a professional skier, and lifeguarding and riding Harley Davidsons in the summer, my days became a living cliché of sex, drugs, and rock 'n roll.

In my opinion, there was only one way to go—full on, top speed—ready to risk my very life for the next thrill. It was the Eighties, when cocaine use was fashionable, not criminal, in certain crowds. I showed up in sketchy places within the drug trade where no one should go, and I met with people no one should see, for the spirit of evil within them was palpable.

I attempted feats so perilous that if I failed, I would have died. One time, perched on a single ski, atop a three-hundred-foot cliff, I stopped yards away from plunging to my death.

My face was a map of cuts and scrapes, and every inch of my back had been bruised or lacerated—the markings of a young man trying to prove himself to a father who didn't care. But the biggest scars were on my heart.

When I found out I could make better money in construction than lifeguarding, I left the slopes of Utah to form a little construction company back home in Minnesota.

By age twenty-seven, I had fifteen men working for me, building high-end, custom homes on golf courses. Enjoying the new income, I purchased my family home on a waterfront and decorated it with a boat, expensive cars, and motorcycles.

I was young, in shape, arrogant, and everything I tried to do I could do well. This world shouted success at me through my possessions, money, power, popularity—not to mention girlfriends.

In time, I got engaged to my trophy girl—the prettiest and wealthiest one of them all. To add to her good qualities, she could pound booze almost as hard as I could and liked the same stuff on pizza.

So that was my life before God changed everything.

Then, one day, at age thirty and in perfect health, a large nail gouged my face in a construction accident, and it required stitches. In reaction to the anesthesia that was used, my body went into anaphylactic shock—and I died.

For two and a half hours, I was gone, cold to the touch.

My body was going to be shipped to an organ harvesting center in Saint Paul, where they would pronounce me brain dead and harvest my organs. I have AB positive blood, a type found in less than two percent of the population, so I am very valuable in parts.

Dead on the hospital bed, suddenly my arm shot out and wrapped around my startled mom and fiancé. I was sitting up and talking, completely healthy in no time.

In the two and a half hours that my body was dead, my soul was in the very presence of God. Soon after, I was shown that if I not been brought back to life, I would have gone to hell for eternity. (More on this later.)

Needless to say, I came back a changed man. The Lord let me know, without compromise or uncertainty, that I was not the lord of my life. He was.

His Mother also reached out to me in an invitation to go to one of her pilgrimage sites, a place called "Medjahoochee," or "Medgegookie." I then read a book by Fr. Joseph Pelletier on the first five days of the apparitions in the small town of Medjugorje in Bosnia-Herzegovina, and was not at all skeptical.

If something this incredible is going on in the world today, I thought, *I want to be like the apostle Thomas and go put my fingers in the Lord's wounds.* I wanted to *touch* Mary's presence. I'd heard about Fatima and Lourdes and other sites of Marian apparitions, but they were far away and long ago. The Medjugorje apparitions began in 1981.

Are they still happening? I wondered. I soon found myself traveling with my mother to this unpronounceable place across the world.

On the first evening after we arrived, on a bench outside the parish church, I found myself listening to the lilting sounds of the Rosary coming through the loudspeaker in Croatian, followed by dozens of different languages harmonized into one voice:

"Holy Mary, Mother of God, pray for us sinners now and at the hour of our death. Amen."

In the middle of the Rosary, at 6:40 pm, the church bells rang out the Ave Maria, announcing the arrival of the Mother of God, whom the locals affectionately call Gospa.

Mary is appearing now on earth to one of the visionaries, I thought to myself. Then all went quiet, extremely quiet, and the atmosphere grew still.

People from around the globe, from Asia, Africa, Europe, and America—wearing cameras, robes, jackets, loafers, and tennis shoes—started to look up and point toward the sky. Joining them, I stood transfixed as I watched the sun shimmer and throb and shoot off beams of light. At intervals, its center turned opaque, with the outside spinning in one direction, then the other, displaying changing and swirling colors.

After a few minutes, I diverted my eyes, realizing I was not supposed to be able to stare at the sun without going blind. I even looked for a bright spot in my vision, which naturally comes from optic fatigue. It wasn't there.

To the woman next to me, I asked, "Do you see that?"

"Yes, the sun is spinning!" she exclaimed, and then I learned that women describe colors differently than men. Purple, as far as I knew, could be light purple or dark purple.

"It's lavender!" she began. "No wait, it's turning violet, now mauve. Actually, more like mulberry or magenta…"

As she continued to name all the colors on a paint wheel, I wanted to share this with my mom, so I began walking toward the back of the church along a pea-gravel path in search of her. At the point when I stood directly outside of where the Tabernacle resided inside the church, I was suddenly taken away…and shown my life.

✟   ✟   ✟

I saw all the sinful events of my life up through the present moment. It was an illumination of conscience, an experience more intimate and vivid than a movie, more realistic than a 3-D image. I had the sense God was there, somewhere behind me, watching everything.

I was aghast to learn the implications of my sin, how my actions or inactions were so much bigger than a single event, and had a ripple effect on others across time and into eternity. I had no idea that human beings were related in this way.

Bawling uncontrollably, all I could say over and over again was, "I'm sorry. I'm so sorry. I didn't know."

But it was clear I had a choice in every situation. And I chose poorly. The first scene God showed me was of myself as a five-year-old boy, reaching up to steal a Matchbox car on a store rack, and I felt how it broke God's heart. He loved me beyond all telling and would have given me anything.

At the same time, God communicated the intricacies of deliberation that went into my choice. At that tender young age, I knew that taking the car was wrong. I knew my parents or my grandmother would have happily paid for it. I had no reason to steal it. God revealed to me all the things we never think of. *It's just a toy car. What could it hurt anybody?*

But my small action hurt relationships of trust. Insurance had to pay. The owner of the store had to pay. His and others' trust in their fellow human beings was further eroded, which changed their behavior—and so on, and so on.

The theft had an effect on me, as well. There was the loss of innocence. Once I performed that deed, I could never take it back. It could be confessed and forgiven, restitution might be made, but a reality would still hold that would remain part of my experience. And that could never be changed. But after I stole it, I did not repent, and therefore every subsequent theft became that much easier.

Then I saw, in mind-boggling detail, scenes of my moral descent into all the world and the devil had to offer.

At first, my conscience knew there was an undeniable self-ishness attached to my transgressions because I was created and taught to know better. But as my sins grew progressively worse, my conscience became ever more muted, until in time, the voice of truth in my life was either actively ignored or shut out completely.

Materialism, power, and pleasures became my gods. I saw my attachment to the forty-foot yacht, the giant house on the river, the cool cars, the fancy clothes, the sex, the drugs. Not once did I think of consequences because consequences were not apparent to me. Without experiencing most of the negative effects of my actions and rationalizing away any that did come, I made my pursuits acceptable in my own mind.

Embracing the mentality of the world today, I believed if they didn't catch me, didn't charge me, and didn't bring me before the magistrate, then what I was doing was okay. God was giving me immediate, intimate knowledge of this folly. He exposed my own cherished lies and those I had embraced from society.

For example, if abortion was legal and contraception was available, weren't these things okay? No. If politicians make marijuana legal and call it medicinal, that makes it okay, right? No. These were lies. What really matters is what God thinks, what God says. I chose to be ignorant of God.

I believed the damning lie that because two people consent to a sexual act, it is therefore justified. With each encounter I had with a woman, I was fully responsible for my part and partially responsible for hers. The degrees of culpability and the far-ranging, rippling repercussions were different for each act and each person.

Sometimes a woman wanted to please me because she had every intention of having a deep relationship that involved marriage, yet I had no intention of commitment whatsoever.

Even when my intentions were better, my sin was still sin. I could never give back what I had taken from so many women. Sometimes this included taking their virginity, which was crushingly serious—worse than beating them.

If I had run after them and apologized a thousand times, their relationships with men throughout their lives would still be negatively affected, not to mention their eternal souls.

Every one of my sexual sins, like all sin, involved pain and suffering, but I hadn't allowed myself to see the dire repercussions of my choices.

My mother wanted me to act differently toward women, but I pretended to be cavalier and uncaring about her feelings, which was not the truth. During my illumination, I felt her pain within myself. She was so disappointed. Long before she moved into my home, she would visit and try her best to help me, but I insisted that she tolerate my behavior in exchange for a relationship with me. It was against her sensibilities, so she did not accept it, yet she still loved me anyway.

My response was to reject her physically and emotionally.

"I'm not coming over to your house. I'm not seeing you!" I bellowed.

This was the woman who bore me into the world, who loved me, whom God had chosen as my mother. Reliving this moment, I felt the slicing pain of rejection that had stabbed my mother's heart to its core.

Even choices that did not seem serious to me were indeed serious, and my good intentions were never enough to cover them up. When someone passed me a joint at a rock concert, for instance, even if I didn't intend to do drugs when I was there, I still bore the responsibility for my choice to take a hit, however disinterestedly.

One event with my fingerprints all over it was profoundly disturbing. I sold drugs to a certain guy on several occasions, then moved away and never saw him again. Later, a man at a local tavern told me that the guy had committed suicide. In the illumination of conscience, I was shown the event of his death.

It is still hard for me to accept and to know that in certain and real ways, I was part of his decision-making process to end his life on earth. In seeing the ripple effects of my sin, I learned that he was holding his family together. When he died, he crushed each member of his family. Their suffering, in turn, afflicted every relationship they had with others, and so on, in a spiral of pain.

All of the sinful events of my life passed before my eyes and through my emotions, in the eternal presence of God, where there could be no deception, no rewriting of history, no mitigation of circumstances. It was what it was. All the false versions of my history were being erased and my guilt was being exposed.

Like most human beings, I had rewritten the unconfessed sins of my past, creating skewed interpretations in my mind to downplay any personal culpability and disperse blame away from myself. I had decimated every one of the Ten Commandments. Intense remorse flooded my soul. I felt devastated by the heavy weight of truths about myself that I did not want to see, did not want to feel, did not want to own. People had died because of my actions. I witnessed moments in my life that I could barely believe were my own.

Mortified, I just wanted to go away, to curl up and die, but I couldn't escape. I believe if I had been shown the condition of my soul without the merciful support of God, I would have experienced a despair so great that I would have died.

✝   ✝   ✝

When I came out of the illumination, I found myself kneeling and looking up at the miracle of the sun, still spinning and pulsating with color. I glanced downward to see the front of my shirt and the flagstones beneath me wet with tears.

A few feet away, sitting on a bench, was my mother. I could see from her posture that she, too, could see this miracle of the sun, so I stood up, walked behind her, wrapped my arms around her, and rested my chin next to her cheek.

Together we looked up at the most powerful energy source known to man, which God had created and was manipulating because he is not bound by the natural laws he designed. In the presence of such a miracle, we were like little kids cuddled up in innocent awe, observing the power of God.

It then occurred to me that I had experienced the whole of my life in the same few short minutes that Mary, the Mother of God, had appeared on earth. *How could it be*, I wondered, *that scarcely any time has passed?*

So that was my first day in Medjugorje.

The next day, I woke up with an all-consuming desire to go to Confession. I walked through the mist and rain toward Saint James Church, underneath scattered clouds.

Sitting down on a wet bench, I thought to myself, *I would have liked to confess to Fr. Mike Canary,* an Irish priest I had met the night before. He had become a priest later in life. I had sensed from his demeanor that he would understand the gravity of my sins and would give me a harder penance than a few Hail Marys.

I did not think of my ponderings as prayer, but no more had I finished my thought than Fr. Mike walked into view!

For the next three hours, we sat together on that bench, huddled under his umbrella, as I told him my sins. Like Saint Padre Pio, he could read into my soul; he knew the details of my sins before I could say them. When I had difficulty admitting my most shameful and embarrassing moments, he would help me by reminding me of the particulars. "And this is what you were doing," or "But this is what you were thinking."

When I finally finished, he gave me my penance. "You go to the mountain, the Mountain of the Cross. You take your shoes off, not as a penance, but an equalizer for all the infirm and elderly, the sick and the less able who come here. You are young and strong, and you climb that mountain in your bare feet, and you pray for every person you've ever hurt."

Then he laid his hands on my head for absolution, and heat came out of them and into me. I didn't know what it was. I just knew that it was.

Then I climbed the mountain. I could remember the name of every person I hurt. I could remember the lies, the thefts, the cheating, the seductions. I sobbed all the way to the top, and because my shoes at the bottom, I sobbed even more all the way down.

At the base of the mountain, there is a crucifix. I prostrated myself and begged Jesus for my life. I knew that even if I could walk this life perfectly from that moment forward, I would never be able to make up for all the harm I had done.

When I finally stood back up, I felt truly forgiven. I had never felt that way before in my life. I put my shoes back on and thanked God for his extravagant mercy.

Then I walked back to the church, where I ran into Fr. Mike again. I followed him into a room with rows of metal folding chairs and people singing hymns. It a healing service. I didn't know what that meant and did not think I necessarily needed one. I was happy and I felt forgiven.

What could it hurt?

Fr. Mike pulled out a purple stole, put it around his neck, and walked to the front of the room. People stood up one at a time and walked over to him.

When my turn came, and I was in front of him, my mouth opened involuntarily, and I heard myself say, "I have many scars on my heart, and what I want is the Holy Spirit."

Putting my hand over my mouth incredulously, I thought, *Okay, that was weird. I wasn't gonna say anything.*

Fr. Mike didn't utter a word. He picked up a small vial of holy oil, made the sign of the cross on my forehead, put his right hand on my head and then on my heart.

Suddenly the Holy Spirit descended with great force, and I was afraid, not from fear, but awe. The Spirit stopped right above my heart. The experience was more than psychological, physical, spiritual, or emotional, and it dwarfed any human drug or sexual pleasure. It was the most explosively powerful event of my life.

Father then told me, "Let there be no more doubt. Let there be no more fear," and in that moment, my spirit expanded, as though taking in the biggest breath of air possible. The more I opened myself, the more God filled me, until there was no distinction between him and me.

When I finally returned to awareness of my surroundings, I found myself lying on the floor. Father Mike had his hand on my heart and was praying over me along with a young man named Bill Curry, who six months earlier had been a drunk before God delivered him from his addiction in Medjugorje.

My feet were sticking straight out and my body was stiff, as though it had been jolted with a million volts. I could have easily served as a plank across the folding chairs.

Gradually, as my body began to relax, a delightful warmth entered my soul. I had been happy before, when winning the big game, falling in love, achieving success, and celebrating Christmas, but I'd never known true joy.

When I got up, I embraced Fr. Mike, who said I hugged him so hard I almost broke his back. I couldn't help it. I loved him! I loved everybody! It was sappy.

I didn't care.

The experience so filled me with the Spirit of God that I could feel my heart beating with love for all of his creatures. It so cleansed my soul that I could almost sense people's bad thoughts. I walked outside into the cold with just a t-shirt and a smile. I did not need my sweater because I was emanating intense heat.

So that was my second day in Medjugorje.

The next day was the Feast of Corpus Christi, celebrating the Body of Christ in the Eucharist. At dawn, as I lay in bed, I experienced another mystical event. This time, I found myself standing in a field of tall grass with a wooden fence on my left, which trailed down a slope before me. A soft wind blew waves through the grass, making the underside of the blades appear silver in the sunlight.

Then Jesus came. He walked up the slope and stopped a few feet in front of me, between me and the fence.

He looked exactly like I would have expected. The only image I have seen that resembles his face was captured by a young artist named Akiane Kramarik, who has, without any training whatsoever, miraculously painted like a master since her childhood.

The face of Jesus she painted was the face I beheld. He wore a soft, cream-colored garment flecked with brown, under a dark brown robe with banded strands of four or five threads woven in a checkered pattern. I could clearly make out his bearded face and his intense, but inviting eyes.

Then without speaking, Jesus communicated to me:

I want you to be a priest.

I was completely taken aback.

"You've got to be kidding. I am the worst sinner ever, and we've just been through this!"

"Yes," he responded.

"But I'm engaged to be married. I love my fiancée. I've already picked out names for my kids. The dress is bought. The country club is rented. Critical mass has been achieved. And sorry, but I've been treating her like my wife already."

I had never, ever, ever, *ever* thought of being a priest—never one moment of altar boy fervor. No inclination, nothing, not one single time.

"Yes," Jesus repeated.

"C'mon. This isn't for guys like me. That's for someone else. You create those guys. You know from beyond time that they're going to be priests. You put them in a wonderful family, they come out the altar boy chute, and then—boom— they're priests."

"I know what I'm doing," He said, then turned and walked away.

Rick Wendell did become a Catholic priest. Listen to the rest of his testimony online or read it (along with other moving testimonials) in Christine Watkins' book, **Of Men and Mary,** *available at QueenofPeaceMedia.com.*

Sister Nicolina Kohler

I grew up a nice Catholic girl in a quaint town in Germany. Playful and flirtatious, without much religious depth, I made fun of nuns in their habits, calling them traffic obstacles and walking chapels. But God's sense of humor is better than mine, because at age nineteen I entered the Dominican sisters of Oakford to become a nun in full habit.

My order eventually assigned me to northern California, which has been my home ever since. I was placed in charge of postulants, then candidates, and finally novices. In my own estimation and that of my community, I was a good nun who loved God and prayer and people.

In 1984 I celebrated my twenty-fifth year as a nun and was granted a sabbatical. Wanting to gain more insight into Scripture, I enrolled in Ecce Homo University in Jerusalem.

Our study included excursions to places where pivotal events occurred, such as the Garden of Gethsemane and the Church of the Last Supper. But there was one place I did not want to go: Church of the Holy Sepulchre. It is said to be the place of the Lord's burial and resurrection, below the actual ground where he was crucified.

I wasn't interested in Calvary. Each year when Holy Week came, I looked forward to Easter, my favorite. Holy Thursday was fine, but then Good Friday had to come. Couldn't we just skip over the torture? It seemed so hard and horrible. I often wondered why Jesus had to be crucified.

My generation, the youth of World War II Germany, didn't understand the Holocaust. Why didn't those before us stand up for the Jews? We had lost faith in the adults. Never again should war, suffering, and death happen.

And yet it happens anyway. No one can escape misery and death. But after decades of being a nun, I was blind to that. I wanted to make the world better, beautiful and whole, without understanding the necessity of suffering.

I began the semester with over forty students from more than thirty-two countries. One, Ruth, had been teaching at a Lutheran seminary in South Africa. Since my order is based in South Africa, she had met some of the sisters there. This connection helped us become friends. Curious and open, she liked to hear about my Catholic beliefs. Her study focused on the passion of Christ, and her fascination with Calvary had carried her many times to the Church of the Holy Sepulchre along the Via Dolorosa.

One day, Ruth enthusiastically invited me to go there. We needed to leave very early in order to escape the throngs and enjoy the peaceful morning silence.

I hesitated, because I really didn't want to go and hadn't thought about why. I had told myself I wanted to, and would go at a later point when I felt prepared.

Not hearing any response from me, Ruth asked, "Do you have an alarm? We would have to leave here around 3:30 in the morning. I'll arrange everything."

Conflicted, I didn't want to lose face. I was a Catholic nun after all, the only one at the school, and in full habit, at that.

Reluctantly I agreed, secretly hoping to sleep through it all, but at 3:30 am, there was the knock at the door. Darn.

"Sister Nicolina, are you up?"

I opened the door and said tersely, "Yes, I am up."

"We are leaving in exactly ten minutes."

Darn.

We stepped into the dark morning along the paved, upward slope of the Via Dolorosa, the way Our Lord walked toward Calvary. The original road lies far beneath the ground. Ruth stopped at a corner. Looking up, I saw the first Station of the Cross: a shrine with an iron gate, depicting a relief of Our Lord being condemned to death.

She dropped to her knees in the center of the small street. I cringed. Bewildered and upset, I stood there looking at the stark picture of Jesus, watching this mystery envelope Ruth.

My mind raced: *I didn't sign up for this. This wasn't part of the deal. If this is the first station, I hope we're not stopping at thirteen more of these! Let's just get this church visit over with. I sure hope we're done in time for class.*

I already felt reluctant. Now I was fully resistant. There wasn't a prayer in my heart, not a one.

For the next four stations, I just stood there; never knelt, never prayed. Ruth knelt each time and went deep into herself, with her head on the ground or resting gently on the station's image. This wrinkled my brow. *What a spectacle.*

People began filling the street. No one else was acting this way; they were going about their business. This wasn't being done in my way or in my time. *Why couldn't we act normal?*

We came to the sixth station, depicting Veronica wiping Jesus' face with the cloth that took on its imprint. His face shone clearly like on the Shroud of Turin.

This time, when Ruth began to pray, I didn't look her, but at the face of Jesus. Suddenly, his image on the cloth spoke to me through a memory:

On the night before my final vows, I was staying overnight at a retreat center. The only other sister prepared to make vows with me was seized with great doubts. I remembered how ready I felt to give my life completely to the Lord, how I longed to give my lifetime vow for him. I was worried she might run off and cause the ceremony to be canceled. I felt like a woman on the night before her wedding day, unsure if it would even take place.

Throughout that night, I could barely sleep because the other sister's turmoil. As dawn cast the first ray of light across my bed, I opened my eyes to see the image on the wall of Jesus's face on the Shroud of Turin. I hadn't noticed it before.

His eyes were closed, but as I continued looking, he literally opened them half way. He focused directly on me with a long, deep look of love! I actually saw his pupils focus, and his gaze penetrated my soul. It touched me with such an infusion of ecstatic peace and total love that I knew no matter what my sister was going through, all would be well that day, and I would give my life to the Lord.

While I stood on the Via Dolorosa, transfixed by the memory of Jesus' face on the shroud, the Lord's love came into my soul again, so strong and real that I found myself on my knees with my head bowed low, unaware of how it happened. The remaining stations became a real journey up to Calvary. From that moment on, I was no longer walking with Ruth. I was walking with Jesus.

It didn't bother me anymore how long we knelt. I didn't care how we looked. More people passed by, and some even bumped into us. I didn't see them. I was part of Jesus' story.

Then we arrived at the Church of the Holy Sepulchre. The natural geography had been covered over by civilization, but the rocky hill upon which Jesus was crucified remained exposed within structure of the church. Christians had built around it over the centuries. We would be able to touch that same rock with our hands.

We walked inside, heading toward Calvary.

Monks were chanting morning hymns. In somber silence, we waited near where Jesus was nailed to the cross. Ruth knew that the monk guarding the chapel would soon fall asleep. We would have this hallowed place to ourselves.

"That altar in front of us," Ruth whispered, "stands directly over a hole in the rock where the True Cross was inserted. It was specially erected here because an altar is for sacrifice, and this is where *the sacrifice* for us and for our sins took place. But you can't get to where the cross was erected unless you kneel down and crawl under."

She paused for a moment in reverence.

"When you get to the place where Jesus died for you, you have to become very small."

Ruth knelt down and crawled underneath the altar. I could not see what she was doing. Normally the monks only allow a pilgrim a minute or less inside the space. After praying in silence for ten minutes, Ruth came out and gestured for me to come forward.

Not knowing what to expect, I dropped to my knees and lowered my head under the altar. Darkness surrounded me. I reached my hand down into a pitch-black hole in the rock. At that moment, time was suspended.

Whether or not I stayed in my body or traveled out of it, I do not know…

I saw the crucifixion in front of me, even though my eyes were closed. And on the cross was Jesus, nailed alive, looking directly at me. His eyes were soft and kind. They held no condemnation, no desire to complain or punish. They were so filled with love that in the illumination of his gaze, I saw my unworthiness as I never had before.

Held by his look of pure mercy and understanding, I couldn't help but cry and cry over my sins, which were many and repellent. I would have dissolved in a flood of tears if he hadn't wrapped me in his grace and sustained me with his eyes.

The experience felt so big, so overwhelming. I was living a lie in so many ways, yet I did not feel a need to hide or lower my head out of embarrassment or shame, like I would before another human being.

Jesus took off my mask, my outer shell, my painted-on face, so I could see my real self. Stripped naked before him, I didn't feel demeaned or have to cover up anything.

I saw my pride. I saw my life of betrayal, and how much I hurt Jesus and others with each little sin. It all added up to an attitude, a lifestyle.

I didn't see specific moments, but rather a larger picture, which made it more horrible. Jesus remained on the cross in terrible pain, as his penetrating, all-knowing, all-loving stare infused me with interior knowledge. I knew everything about myself all at once, and everything was painfully clear.

He was showing me my soul as he saw it, by bringing into focus the ugliness of my sins with all my excuses erased, so that he could pull me straight to his bosom without any lies or barriers, and so I could rest my head on his heart without any fear or pride.

Jesus did not show me my noble qualities and talents. They still remained in his gaze, precious and good, but he chose not to bring them forward. My gifts, he revealed, were not for selfishness or show, but for service.

I saw how I tried not to make a show of myself, yet wanted to be seen. My self-assertion suddenly appeared devious. I had given it all the right names while denying my real motivation.

I had always mistakenly thought I was not a proud person, and yet I was simply proud in a deceptive way.

Having a colorful personality, I could wiggle my way into the middle of almost any group. If I didn't make it into the center of people's lives, I walked away and became the center somewhere else. When leaving a group behind, I would think to myself, *I don't like them.* This was a judgment born of *the big I*, selfishness, because my vanity had not been satisfied.

If you would have asked me, "Are you proud and vain?" I would have replied with confidence, "No."

In relationships, I was shown how I got my own way, yet not in a pushy manner, but by being cute. People served me very easily, especially when I was young. I was entertaining. I was fun. I had a big smile. But it was all fake and not true virtue. This stood out very clearly, and it was ugly.

Growing up, my siblings had to suffer from my selfishness. My eldest sister always had to pick up after me because I never followed through with anything having to do with work.

I told God what I told everyone, "I am not made for work. I am made for fun."

My brothers would say to me, "You aren't beautiful like a cover girl, but you have personality. You can wind men around your little finger, then take off like a butterfly."

"Oh, no. That isn't true. I would never want anyone around my little finger," I would reply, while basking in the swarms of attention.

I never saw myself as jealous, either. I never understood that sin. If someone else was getting all the attention, I didn't bother getting jealous. *Well,* I would think, *he's not the only person in the world,* and I would go find someone else to adore me.

The Lord showed me my temper. When I got very angry, I would shoot people to the moon in my mind. *Wow,* I would sometimes tell myself, *there are so many people up there on the moon now. The sky is full! I'd better cut this out. Maybe one day someone might shoot me there, and then I'll have to spend eternity with them!*

Cutting through my ego, Jesus revealed my devious shortcomings in religious life as well. As a young nun, I believed

I could become holy quickly if I followed all the Dominican rules and regulations. I made an idol of my religious practice. Thinking I was somehow holy by following all the rules also reduced my idea of holiness to *no big deal*. At the root of my perception was pride, which creeps stealthily in to destroy all good deeds.

I fooled myself, thinking I was doing all the right things, while in truth I was breaking rules all the time. For example, the sisters had to be in convent with lights out by 10:00 pm. Yet sometimes I pretended to go down to the chapel in order to watch a movie in the recreation room after hours.

After compline prayers, profound silence was expected until the next morning, yet at times, a few of us would sit out in the car chatting instead. I made excuses like, "I wasn't in the house, so the rule didn't apply to me."

My inward deception helped me think of myself as following the rule perfectly and with my heart. I was never guilty. *I'm a good nun.*

We sisters abandoned strict rules after the Second Vatican Council in the Sixties. Yet Jesus showed me that breaking the ones still in place was a sin. I had taken a vow of obedience before God, period.

As for gluttony, I rarely overindulged, but Jesus reminded me that I had snacked all my life, which is not the point of convent life. In the poverty of our order, there is never much extra food around. The convent rules say you should not eat outside of mealtimes unless you're ill.

I was brazen. "This is not a hidden sin," I jokingly told the sisters in California. I loved to open the fridge at night in search of anything left to snack on, and had my excuses ready.

Additionally, the Lord showed me my many other attachments: to position, planning, people, and attention; and to my own ways, opinions, and desires.

When people upset my plans, my mood grew sour, because my excellent agendas, which were always perfect and without wiggle room, were being changed.

My gift of intertwining my heart with my mind became a problem when I took things personally. In a meeting, I could hold a strong opinion.

If someone with a stronger voice said, "No way, Nicolina," I felt personally offended because my ideas felt like part of my own heart.

When I was younger, respecting my older superiors came easy. But over time, as younger sisters climbed the ranks, I sometimes treated them as though they were still my novices and indulged in power struggles.

By God's grace and through no merit of my own, I easily outshined the other sisters in my good works, never thinking anything was amiss. The Lord showed me my error: I made my abilities the measure for other people, believing, *What I can do, you can also do.* My standard of judgment was *me*.

Jesus showed me another fault. I would get quite piqued when I heard others say untrue things about me. I believed I had to defend myself vigorously and tell everyone the way things really were. Highly offended and lacking in charity, I was quick to correct any misquote or misinterpretation.

Jesus disliked this. Instead, he desired a different response: "Lord, you know what I said, did, or meant, so I do not have to justify myself because you are more important. You know everything."

Why did I need to correct people about myself? The Lord does want us to defend ourselves against abuse or a misjudgment that would cause serious harm. But he knows the truth, he is the judge—no one else, and usually, that is enough.

As the insights continued, one after another, Jesus brought to light my indignation over people saying things that *were actually true* about me. For example, the sisters often pointed out when I was flirting.

I would say, "Why is this guy always hanging around me?"

"You don't see the way you're looking at him and flirting with him?" they would reply.

In denial, I would call it "being friendly." I was perfect, you see, so why were they making me out to be imperfect?

I was also shown how I had to free myself from attachment to friends. Once again, one of my strengths, my love for intimate connections with people, was also my weakness. People walked easily into my heart, and I allowed them to push Jesus further out. I could easily wrap my thoughts and time around someone and then acknowledge Jesus only once in a while. But the Lord wanted my primary focus to always be on him. In him was everything I needed.

I had a cardiac condition and had to learn how to control my emotions so as not to aggravate my illness, yet under the altar of sacrifice at Calvary, I lost all emotional control. My conscience seized my heart with inexpressible torment, and only by crying uncontrollably could I release it.

My tears flowed not from embarrassment, but from seeing the suffering on the Lord's body and face due to *my* sins.

"This is all for you," his eyes said. "I did this all for you."

His words thrust a fiery sword through my heart, causing a searing, stabbing pain. I wanted to die, and yet didn't, because I longed to be worthy of the love in his eyes.

I had never experienced the agony of my own sins before. I had always explained them away. Jesus loved me to the point of death, and I had not tried very much at all to love him in return. I had snuck around in side-stepping, slippery ways, which meant that the way I had lived my life was hypocritical. What hurt the most was my realization that I was projecting the appearance of being a saint while not being one.

So much transpired during my mystical encounter with the crucified Jesus that I lost track of time. At least two hours had passed when I finally crawled out from underneath the altar. I emerged with an indelible mark of unworthiness on my soul, and with an unshakable knowledge of being sublimely loved and adored. How one can receive both at the same time, only God knows.

I missed my class but didn't care. Ruth had already gone back to the university after waiting a half hour, realizing that something special was going on beneath that altar.

Jesus had chosen to give me the greatest graces not in a site I felt drawn to, like Bethlehem or Nazareth, but at Calvary. Nowhere was I so profoundly touched as in the place where I was most reluctant to go.

People often say to me, "Oh, you are a good nun."

Don't believe it. We cannot go by what people say, good or bad. We have to look at Jesus Christ, and then we know who we really are.

The Lord touched the deepest places in me and changed me. These are moments we cannot receive on our own. They can only come through the Lord's gaze.

Now when my wishes and desires are not met, when life is hard and painful, I can lock glances with Jesus and bring meaning and purpose to it all, and not run away. I can unite my own little crosses with his, and suffer them with him, in him, and for him.

Many times I have reflected on that day with Ruth. It was our journey to Calvary that turned my heart around. No longer was Good Friday a day to avoid. Now I want to lengthen it. I want to enter more profoundly into Jesus's suffering and ponder at length his great love, all because of what I beheld in his eyes. Those eyes.

Marino Restrepo

I was born in a small town in Columbia called Anserma, high in the Andes mountains. Both my grandfathers were powerful patriarchs who owned coffee plantations, so my immediate and extended family members are coffee growers.

My mother gave birth to ten children, eight of whom are living, and I am the sixth; two of my older brothers died very young. My uncles and aunts were even more prolific with fifteen to twenty children each, which gave me ninety-two immediate cousins. Our family is more like a tribe, and our Catholicism extends back many generations, so I never had to search for God or for a friend.

When I was fourteen I was sent to Bogotá, the capital, to finish high school. It was the 1960s, and many of my friends were walking away from the Catholic faith. So did I. It was easy to leave, and there was no one telling us to do otherwise.

At sixteen, I fell in with a group of American hippies visiting Colombia for three months. One was a young blue-eyed American girl named Donna. She introduced me to marijuana, liberation from the establishment, and everything she knew about sex—and I stopped believing in God.

From marijuana, I quickly graduated to LSD, mescaline, PCP, and mushrooms, and then to dealing all of them. I also dove headfirst into eastern paganism, tarot cards, occultism, metaphysics, gurus, magic, divination—to all the spiritually poisonous occult practices which eventually became known as the New Age movement.

In the course of four years, I had affairs with innumerable Donnas who were visiting from all over the United States, and with a similar number of Marias from my own country.

In the late 1960s, I ended up living with a Colombian girl for a full year without having other relationships, something abnormal for my new lifestyle. She and I seemed to be meant for each other. When I was twenty, I got her pregnant.

Most of her family was involved in politics, working for the government and had a lifestyle our generation despised. Her family, in turn, considered us the trash of the world. We got married in a Catholic church in Bogotá, even though we did not believe in marriage anymore, because we both had Catholic parents who demanded it.

A few days after the ceremony, her relatives suggested we move to Germany, where they would help us find work. The truth was, they wanted to send us far away from them so we could not damage their reputation.

In Germany I studied at the University of Hamburg and became an actor and musical composer. We lived there for a little over six years, and my wife gave birth to two sons. By the end of our stay, the only pastime my wife and I shared as a couple was our outings to expensive rock concerts, which we attended after our babies were fed. This left us without adequate funds for everything else, but we didn't care.

Although we cared for one another and knew each other intimately, the union between us changed. She started to feel nostalgic for her roots while I became increasingly involved in my artistic, psychedelic world. We returned to Colombia in 1976 and we separated soon after.

I left for the United States and spent some time in Florida and New York doing theater. With a heart riddled with anxiety, due to the separation from my children and wife, I immersed myself into a confused and troubled world of bars, cocaine, and women as decadent as I was.

Two years later, my artistic connections and acquaintances in New York led me to move to Hollywood, California. The same spirit that had baptized me into Donna's world through sex and drugs continued to guide my life with force.

For the next twenty-nine years I worked as an actor, composer, director, and producer while roving within a Hollywood mecca of drugs, lust, and the New Age.

In the mid-Seventies, while living in Hollywood, I signed with CBS Records and traveled to many countries with a band, promoting music and producing records.

I had money, fame, and power, and truly believed I was the coolest guy in town.

A slave to the New Age, I decorated my home using Feng Shui, an imported Chinese tradition. My sofa faced north, my bed faced south, and my mirror next to the front door reflected a crystal to the right so that everything channelled universal energy correctly.

I cultivated so-called powers, cosmic forces, and esoteric knowledge through candles, astrology, horoscopes, psychics, and so on, in addition to following all the superstitions I had brought from my own culture, plus those I had picked up from the countries I had visited. All was gain in my eyes.

The evil one, being very astute, made sure that everything I touched turned into worldly success so that I would think my esoteric spiritual practices must be right and good. When I visited my Catholic relatives who were suffering financially, I would counsel them to follow my occult practices.

Their response was to cross themselves and run. *These people are so funny,* I'd think. *They're living in the dark ages.*

But I was the one living in the dark all while believing I dwelled in the bright light. It was impossible for me to detect Lucifer, dressed as an angel of light, because I was walking right with him.

The only person able to bring a perspective of God to my life was my mother. When she flew to California to visit, she would tell me, "I'm not impressed with your money or your success. I'm very concerned about your soul. If you die living the type of life you're living, you're going to be condemned."

It was inconceivable to my family that I had lost my faith and didn't believe in Jesus, so upon returning home, my mother would simply tell people, "Pray a lot for Marino."

My mother's warning rang deep within me, but I was not about to pay attention because I had too much on my plate. Besides, Catholics were an outdated breed who had to learn from me. How could they still believe in such things as hell? What a superstitious, dehumanizing, and absurd concept! Whenever the subject came up in conversation, I made sure to voice my views loudly.

A few months after I had signed the record deal, my wife arrived from Colombia on a surprise visit to tell me that she had cancer. The news brought me great sadness.

Despite our separation of several years, we had always enjoyed mutual concern and a close friendship because we knew each so well. There were no secrets between us.

Not long after her visit, we decided it would be better for our two sons, now teenagers, to live with me. My first years with them were very difficult because of my frequent music tours. This new responsibility forced me to abandon most of my destructive habits, except for my occult practices, which I considered harmless.

Never mind how all the superstitions I had adopted meant that my surroundings could suddenly turn menacing. I feared much more than just walking under a ladder or a black cat crossing my path. I had turned into an idiot.

In 1992 I entered a period of loss. That year, my wife died after much suffering. The next year my youngest brother died in a boating accident off the island of Antigua; his body was never found. Six months later, my father passed away from a brain hemorrhage. In 1996 my last living brother shot himself to death during an argument with his wife after consuming alcohol at a party in Bogotá.

At the time, my mother was critically ill, emaciated, and worn out from all the family tragedies. Two months later she died in my arms following a three-hour ecstasy during which she relived and narrated her entire life.

A year later I returned to Colombia for Christmas with my four remaining sisters, all practicing Catholics. At the pace our family was going, it seemed as if God might take the rest of us pretty soon. One of my sisters, who had fallen ill, was convinced she was next. She asked if we could go to church to pray the Christmas novena to the Infant Jesus of Prague, a special devotion that was once widespread throughout the Church and still continues in countries such as Colombia and the Philippines. The novena began on December 16 and would end on December 24, with the Baby Jesus laid ceremoniously in the church manger.

Thirty-three years had passed since I had last stepped foot in a Catholic church, and I did not believe in any of it. I only went to please my sisters, particularly the one who believed she would die soon.

As part of the priest's introduction to the novena, he said, "For the one who prays this novena with devotion and faith, the Baby Jesus will grant a grace."

That caught my greedy attention. *Maybe I can get something out of this child,* I thought to myself.

So I asked the sister sitting next to me, "So, how powerful is this baby?"

She shared with me many testimonials of miracles that occurred because of the novena.

"Sounds good to me."

I had long ago lost any understanding of grace. This Baby Jesus, in my perception, was like magic—yet another occult power offering me good luck and fortune. *I am going to ask the Baby Jesus to change my life,* I decided.

Keeping my plan to myself, I asked this baby to give me the opportunity to retire with a lot of money and live the rest of my life like a king, with at least three women, on an island in Indonesia that I'd seen in photos.

"Do it with a lot of faith," said my sister.

"You bet. You bet," I responded.

I felt convinced the Baby Jesus would answer my petition. Little did I know I was talking to God and he would answer my prayer to change my life, but in his own way.

I finished the novena on Christmas Eve. On Christmas, after partying with friends and relatives, I got into my Land Cruiser at midnight with one of my nephews. Off we drove to my uncle's coffee plantation in order to spend the night. My uncle kept the entrance gate open when he was expecting me, so I was surprised to see it closed when we arrived. I stopped the car, and asked my nephew to step out to open the gate.

Suddenly six hooded men holding machine guns jumped from the darkness. Throwing open the car doors, they pushed my nephew into the rear seat, yanked me out, then tied my hands together behind my back. They pulled a hood over my head, then shoved me into the back seat with my nephew.

All six of them piled into the car, then the driver zoomed out of town at a dangerous speed. When we stopped, four of the hooded men stepped out, bringing me with them. The remaining two drove away with my nephew. (Later I learned they abandoned my car and my nephew at a sugar plantation that same night. I never knew that he was safe, so I went on fearing the worst for him.)

Moving quickly, the men then tied a cattle rope around my waist. One held the rope from the front and another from the back. Then they forced me to run through the mountains throughout the entire night, with my hands still tied behind my back and with the suffocating hood still covering my head.

When we finally stopped, I was dumped in what sounded from the echo like an abandoned farm room. At sunrise, still tied up and hooded, I was shoved into a car and spent the next few hours suffering a bumpy ride, without hands or sight to help brace myself.

"We have to change locations," I heard them say, "because the police and army are looking for him."

Then I was forced to walk again for several hours through the night. This time, I could hear the frightening sounds of the jungle, which added to my sheer panic. The jarring ride had left my body bruised and bloody, the humidity was making it even more difficult to breathe through the hood, and the lack of blood circulation was causing shooting pains in my back and arms.

The alcohol I had consumed during the last three days of Christmas partying had sapped my energy, and each step felt like one move closer to a heart attack.

When this terrifying odyssey through the jungle ended, one of the men threw me into a cave. As my body hit the floor, I heard a commotion of fluttering and quickly realized I was surrounded by hundreds of bats. I did not know which was worse, the smell of the cave or the excrement that covered the rotten floor. If I moved even an inch, the bats were disturbed and their excrement rained down upon me.

Adding to this horror, thousands of bugs began crawling out of the bat excrement and into my clothes, biting me from head to toe. Soon, my whole body was covered with various kinds of insect bites. Some felt like electric shocks, others produced great patches of inflammation, and others caused terrible itching, which I could not scratch with my hands still tied behind me.

On the third day, I started to call for my captors, thinking that they might remove me from the cave, and once outside, I might have a chance to escape. I shouted for them, but my voice almost failed me from fatigue.

After some time, one of the men came, dragged me out of the cave by my feet, and yanked my hood off, leaving me listless on the ground.

"Do you want something to eat?" He asked.

I didn't answer. My eyes, lids swollen from bug bites and blinded by days in complete darkness, took time to open and adjust to light. When they did, I became even more afraid.

Sitting up, I stared over at the cave and saw what looked like a macabre stage of enormous spider webs covered with a greenish slime. Slowly, I began to observe the largest and hairiest spiders I had ever seen. They somehow appeared to know I was looking at them.

Horrified, I noticed I had made a large hole in one of the bigger, thicker spider webs, where I had been laying for the last three days. All I wanted to do was run away and I didn't even care if I got shot. But I could barely stand up, because my circulation was so poor. Then the man put the hood back on and shoved me back into the cave.

Once a day, one of my captors would offer me food, but I refused to eat it because I desperately wanted to die. He explained they were giving me what they scrounged from the jungle because another group that was supposed to pick me up hadn't arrived yet. He did not say who they were waiting for, or what they were planning to do with me, and I did not dare to ask any questions.

With each day, I was growing weaker, angrier, and more desperate. All I wanted was to kill those men, find a way to escape, or just die. Eventually, I decided to try to regain some energy and started to eat and drink the wild fruits, roots, and jungle water they were giving me.

On the fifteenth day they took me out of the cave (I kept track of time until the twenty-first day of my kidnapping). I found myself in the midst of nearly eighty Marxist guerrilla rebels in military uniforms, somewhere between the ages of fourteen to twenty-one.

They were members of the FARC revolutionary group and claimed to have an ideology, but they were really just regular criminals. Immediately, I realized that the army had stopped looking for me because these rebels were now able to move about openly without hiding.

The FARC commander of the camp, about thirty years old, started walking around in circles, making a big show of his power, declaring how I had been purchased from my first captors and that I was to pay his group a high ransom. This, he claimed, was only a small amount of my fortune. They must have assumed I was wealthy because I had been on TV and in movies and was a relative of the prominent coffee plantation owners they had been harassing for years.

This caricature-like commander knew who all my sisters were and went as far as to show me a list of their addresses names and telephone numbers. If I refused to give them the money, he threatened, each of my sisters would be killed one by one. I knew that human life meant nothing to them and that they wouldn't hesitate for a second to follow through with this threat.

Laughter from this pack of malnourished, preying jackals was the response to everything the commander said. During this absurd trial in the jungle night, my emotions oscillated wildly between anger and fear, bravery and despair.

My initial kidnappers belonged to a well-known family from my village, who had failed in the drug-trafficking trade and were paying off debts by kidnapping people. The FARC commander explained how these original kidnappers wanted me dead after the ransom was paid because they were from my hometown and feared I would seek revenge. And because I had seen their faces, my sentence was death.

The commander then ordered me back into the cave. The guerrillas put my hood back on, but this time, they tied my hands in the front, which provided only the slightest relief.

Back in that cave, I felt utterly demolished, with no hope whatsoever of making it out alive.

I thought of my boys who were fearing for my life, who no longer had a father. I thought of my sisters, my entire family, now in danger of being killed. I had literally lost everything.

My existence had turned to ashes. I had hit below the bottom, if there was such a place.

I tried desperately to conjure a power, a guide, anything to sustain me through this agony. I groped for help from the eastern philosophies I had cherished as so deep and wonderful.

But the magic formulas, the metaphysical knowledge of the occult, the mantras, the crystals, the mystical amulets from around the world—all these things that I lived for—were offering me nothing and leaving me spiritually bankrupt.

My mind then traveled back to my early years, as I tried to recall the prayers I had said in church and in school, but I could not even remember the Our Father. *Nothing.*

✟   ✟   ✟

It was at that moment, when I was completely destroyed as a human being, that God palpably came into my life. Throughout the night, for about eight or nine hours, the Lord held me in a mystical embrace as I was taken through an illumination of conscience. This was followed by an extraordinary infusion of his teachings (some of which I will include as I relate what happened during my illumination).

Although I will often use the words, 'the Lord showed me,' when describing what I experienced, only after it ended did I understand the Lord to be its source, because at that time, I did not know who the Lord was.

While still maintaining a grip on reality, and while aware of being in the cave, I entered a mysterious, infinite state, with no sense of time or space. In this realm of vivid awareness, I reviewed my entire life of sin.

Suddenly, I saw myself at age three, speeding a tricycle around the old Spanish-style terrace of my childhood home in Colombia. With a stick in hand, I was whacking the decorative plants and damaging the potted flowers. In the background, I could hear the voice of someone telling me to stop.

Maybe, I'm going insane, I thought in the cave. *At age forty-seven, I'm reliving my life at age three.* Petrified, I began to reconsider. *For three hours before Mom died, she talked about her whole life, and so I must be dying, like my mother.*

Then came this thought: *No, maybe I'm hallucinating because I've been bitten by poisonous insects for fifteen days.*

Something deep within was telling me otherwise, but the answer was too mysterious, too big. None of my rationalizations could withstand my unfolding experience, so I gave up trying understand it. My mind was far from thinking that the illumination was coming from God.

As I witnessed scenes from my childhood, I saw how, step by step, I grew increasingly attached to the external world, abandoning my relationship with the Holy Spirit, who had previously permeated my entire existence.

I saw how profoundly my attachments developed to my environment, material possessions, and the people in my life.

The culture into which I was born had also exposed me to unbridled sexual impurity, and early on, I began to engage in intense sexual activity with myself. I lost a sense of joy, love, and security. I gradually turned into a person who constantly depended on human affection, with an appetite increasingly geared toward my senses and instincts.

As I witnessed my childhood happiness fade, I watched my tongue turn into a weapon. As early as elementary school, I committed a terrible offense against one of my schoolmates who was being teased by other students. I gave him the worst nickname, *Gallo,* which means rooster.

He carried this name throughout his life and had to endure humiliation and persecution from many people, which caused him great anguish.

He grew up suffering from isolation and loneliness, which ultimately purified his soul in a precious way. His purification through suffering caused enormous damage to the souls of all those who had contributed to his holiness, including myself. This may sound confusing, but it is exactly the way I saw it take place.

One could argue that as a schoolboy, I was too young to know better and did not yet have a fully formed conscience. On the contrary, this would be a rationalization because the Lord later shared that *wisdom rings in the soul at the moment of birth,* when the soul first becomes perfectly independent from the mother's womb.

This precludes us from feigning ignorance to justify our evil acts. The soul feels the pain of sin at the very moment a sin is being committed or is even consented to in one's mind. Therefore, I had no excuse.

By the time I was seeing my life at ages eleven, twelve, thirteen, and fourteen, I began to experience an excruciating spiritual pain. For the very first time, I was feeling the agony of sin. This suffering penetrated so deeply into my heart that I would never be able to describe its depths—and I was only approaching my teens.

As a forty-seven-year-old in a cave, who did not believe in sin, I was now feeling all the pain of the wrong I had already committed by my early teenage years. The older I got during the experience, the more devastating the agony, for I had spent the prior thirty-three years of my life steeped in mortal sin.

Not only was I witnessing my sins, but I was also shown every *consequence* of every sin. To explain this reality, I will share a particular scene that I was later shown by the Lord:

A group of people were in line for a bank teller early one morning. For some reason, the teller was working slowly. One of the people in the line became restless and started to complain, cursing the bank, its employees, and then the government. Then other people in line became agitated and also began to grumble, so by the time they eventually met the teller, they too insulted him. As a result, the teller lost his temper and behaved badly for the rest of the day.

The chain of events that developed in the bank spread to other parts of that city, causing a rise in hostility and violence, and then *across the ocean* through telephone calls, generating an incredibly long radius of evil actions. By the end of the day, acts of extreme violence were being committed as a consequence of one person's reaction to a teller not working quickly enough.

If I were the one who started the fire of sin, then I was also accountable for its spreading. To see all of my transgressions passing from one soul to another, like a terrible plague, was beyond devastating.

I saw how the relationship between my God (the Creator) and me (the one created) broke down the moment I believed I had control over my own life. By age fourteen, I was encased in such an edifice of vanity, pretentiousness, and pride that I stopped going to the Sacrament of Reconciliation because I thought it was ridiculous to confess to another human being.

I started making fun of the Church and leading others to do the same. I watched myself put forth absurd arguments to demonstrate how unnecessary it was to be part of the Church. I belittled all Christians, and especially Catholics.

"Just look at those priests! They're a wreck. I'm not going to tell them anything. Who needs a middleman anyway?"

Or, "Hell? What a joke that is! It cannot be possible. God wouldn't create us to go to hell. He would never do that to us."

I saw all of the souls I was meant to serve and evangelize had I stayed in the Church. For the next thirty-three years, I would abandon *all of them*. I had received the great blessing, coupled with the great responsibility, of being raised Catholic, and I did nothing with it.

God also highlighted a particular moment in 1966, when I was fifteen years old. I saw myself in the kitchen of a house in Bogotá in the company of a maid about my age. I had a macho attitude inherited from my ancestors, and it manifested through my cruel, arrogant, and abusive actions toward those over whom I had authority.

I spoke to her harshly, while holding an object in my hand that she was supposed to have cleaned. She stared at the floor, her face flush with misery, and neither protested nor showed a single gesture of resistance or disgust.

My soul was torn apart when I saw this because she had been in one of the most delicate states of her spiritual and emotional life, and my actions led her into deeper pain. She had recently been taken from the countryside where she was born. She was separated from her parents and transferred to the big city where she was placed in the service of strangers who felt no love or charity toward her, causing her greater suffering and despair.

I could see how spiritually handicapped I was by the age of sixteen due to the extensive roots I had sunk into the world.

My life had been absolutely drab and filled with anxieties and the desires of nature. With infinite sadness I was witnessing how my sins had caused a separation from the grace that had been given to me at birth.

At age seventeen I entered the territory of the truly fallen, descending into a cavern of impurity via the consummation of my first sexual act with Donna.

Jesus later revealed to me that through fornication, I lost the grace of my baptism and fell back into original sin. It was as if I had never been baptized. Not only was I immersed into the consequences of my own serious sin, but I also received the iniquities of *my ancestors* who had likewise engaged in fornication.

Instead of reserving virginity and chastity for sacramental matrimony between a man and a woman, with its abundance of Christian graces, my ancestors and my culture had chosen the path of carnal pleasure prior to marriage.

Now, so had I.

I was therefore left without a spiritual compass and contributed to multiplying these sins—this horrifying curse—for future generations after me.

From that first act with Donna, my entire life began to function in the flesh and away from the spirit. I saw how my eyes changed and hungered to penetrate the deepest abyss of sexuality. Like sponges, they sought to absorb every detail. As a result, I lost countless graces and the treasure of peace.

If only Our Lord would allow you, the reader, to observe for an instant what I witnessed concerning what the arrival of Donna represented in my life and hers. To see this would be an intense warning as to the seriousness of the battle being fought for our souls.

With horror, during my illumination I followed the growth of my carnal appetite, which brought serious consequences to my life and to those around me. I grew convinced that sex was like breathing.

But the Lord would later explain to me that sexuality is not a need but rather a function. A human can survive without a sexual life. He may not procreate, but he surely will not die or become atrophied, physically, emotionally, or spiritually.

Sexual impurity, he taught me, is one of the fastest routes to separate us light years from his presence, a path that gravely compromises us with its diabolical realms. Every sinful sexual act is an internal metamorphosis, gradually emptying a human being of its spiritual existence. This can only lead the soul to a premature death by turning a person into a walking corpse, driven by the evil one toward an eternal burial.

That first relationship with Donna was the beginning of a long sequence of infernal events in my life. Through her, two different venoms were injected into me: one of hallucinatory drugs and the other of promiscuity, whose poisonous flames were fanned by intergenerational inheritance and my history of masturbation. Uniting with Donna ignited a fire that would not be extinguished for decades.

The devil prepared me well for the coming of my second affair with another visiting American, Cindy. After establishing a fountain of corruption within the two of us, Satan used us as his tools to ensnare those with whom we would come into contact.

Cindy and I caused the destruction of many souls. Through us, others were initiated into LSD and a spontaneous, casual sexual life.

To see all this was extremely painful. Cindy, herself, died of a heroin overdose back home in San Francisco.

The Lord later explained to me that the evil one knows the gifts and talents God has given us. Satan wants to capture all of these capacities for his territory early on in our lives. Otherwise, they will become weapons used against him.

The devil gave me talents to cultivate the opposite sex and I was captivated with ease by women's invitations of carnal passion. Without effort, I could seduce others and could be seduced even more easily.

I saw how I even took on the mannerisms and gestures of the demons working through me. Donna, Cindy, and I were not just puppets of Satan. We were fully conscious of acting against everything addressed in the moral law of God.

After reviewing the truth of my relationships with these two women, I witnessed the evil one using me for many more years, taking advantage of my vitality and artistic inclinations.

From a young age, I had an affinity for the arts, and every artistic talent that I possessed was used by evil to increase the venomous influence of my actions.

It was terribly difficult for me to learn in this revelation that the key to heaven wasn't power, comfort, or sensuality, but renunciation. The world I created for myself was oriented toward avoiding pain and attaining pleasure at any price. My version of reality made it all the more impossible, as every day passed, to conceive that the path of purification toward absolute union with God was paved with suffering, pain, and tribulation.

Moreover, I was chasing happiness in this world. This is an impossible task, because we cannot ever have full realization of the eternal in that which is not permanent. It is like trying to build a house on the waves of the ocean.

At least a thousand times during this illumination I noticed the way my gaze had been riveted on crucifixes in so many places. With my every view of a crucifix, a burning call stirred deep within me but could never reach my heart, because I was immune to the movements of the Holy Spirit.

The more sins I committed, the more tormented I became, and the more desperately I went searching for lost happiness. In the midst of my distress, I ended up doing certain things that a part of me detested most:

God also allowed me to see how, in the midst of my most intensely sinful activity (when I thought I was enjoying the most pleasure physically), my soul was bleeding rivers of internal pain that consumed my entire being. My eyes looked like windows of sadness, covered in carnival makeup, fooling no one.

I also saw the eyes of those who had sinned with me. They, too, were undergoing an interior anguish, with the exception of those who seemed to be completely consumed by darkness.

In the midst of all this pain, the Lord later showed me that he was there in every action, no matter how dark, to alleviate the weight of sin from our tormented souls, which recognized something was totally wrong.

There is no way I can describe to you the spiritual torture I went through in this awakening of my conscience.

I am not sure how I lived through it. I do know that if a person in a state of ongoing mortal sin were to undergo what I experienced, he or she would most likely die.

Throughout this review of my life of sin, I was mysteriously aware that I was still present in the cave. I still possessed a grip on reality. But then that grip was gone. All of a sudden, I was taken into another dimension.

Whether I fainted, died, or fell asleep, I do not know.

I found myself immersed in the freshness of a friendly field, face down in beautiful grass, which covered the plateau of what appeared to be a high mountain, yet one unlike any on earth.

I was amidst the most incredible and immense silence, what I will call, *the perfect silence.* I could also see my body in that cave in another dimension.

My first thought was, *I just died.* And yet I had never felt so alive. My entire being was weightless, free from all anxiety or pain and permeated with a pure sense of joy. Before me far in the distance, I noticed another even higher mountain, disconnected from the one I was on.

Through a distant mist surrounding the mountaintop, a spectacularly beautiful city slowly emerged. I was in a perfect state of knowledge, understanding everything I was seeing.

I began to explore this city. I could see it inside and out, even though it was distant. I knew perfectly well that my soul was supposed to have ended up there, but had not made it.

Then I heard the voice of the Lord speak to me. I knew it was God. His voice sounded so majestic, so immense, that it seemed to come from everywhere in the universe, while at the same time, from inside of me.

All of the beauty in the world could not begin to describe it. I was experiencing the most magnificent, loving, forgiving, compassionate voice, but in my pride, I felt so ashamed of being who I was in the presence of this awesomely magnanimous God that I wasn't able to accept his mercy. I wanted to sink into my shame, but the Lord kept holding me up.

He was trying to save me from myself. The more shame I experienced, the more mercy and love he showed me in a back-and-forth symphony for my salvation. The unconditional love and extravagant mercy in the Lord's voice was burning me. I did not want to hear it, so I turned it down. People have a hard time thinking that we human beings could ever reject God, who only wants to save us. But we can.

This happens if we die and appear before the Lord without love. When I rejected the Lord's voice, he immediately stopped talking to me. I fell into an indescribable loneliness. The silence was no longer perfect, but instead became the total absence of love. I knew that if that voice did not talk to me again, I would be destroyed, because that voice was my life.

Then everything vanished: the grass, the mountains, the city of light. I was floating on top of a terrifying abyss, above what appeared to be an ocean of fog. I began to sink into it, and as I descended, I noticed that it wasn't fog at all.

Every particle was a condemned soul, a demonized person. Each horrifying figure still possessed traces of being human; I could see the resemblance of an arm, the piece of a face. But every being was totally deformed by sin, and I was perfectly aware of exactly what type of sin had inflicted what type of deformity. At the same time, I also knew and felt the origin of every one of my own terrifying deformities.

As I looked deeper into this frightening abyss in the bowels of the earth, I saw that it became increasingly complicated because there were *infinite* levels of condemnation, and all of the condemned human souls were connected to demonic hierarchies far below. And those hierarchies were formed by fallen angels.

Each hierarchy was ruling a different territory of sin and I could see how souls were eternally enslaved to the hierarchies of demons that corresponded with their sins. It was as if the souls were wired to them. And I was wired to them, too. My sins were perfectly connected to millions of evil spirits in different dimensions of the abyss.

All at one time I saw the horrifying faces of the demons I had fornicated and committed adultery with! I saw the evil, twisted faces of my violence, dishonesty, greed, and gluttony.

Most people who are living in mortal sin, as I was, argue God is merciful, therefore there is no hell.

Well, I was wrong. There is a hell.

Surrounded by abominable creatures beyond my wildest imaginings, I experienced the most excruciating pain of my whole human existence. I felt as though my soul was stolen, raped, and trampled on.

The worst part was recognizing I had voluntarily caused this. Even though the word rape might sound exaggerated, I truly sensed a violation of the inner recesses of my soul. I could see the different angles in which evil worked in me and how it had invaded the spaces of my inner life, gradually erasing the minutest details of the presence of God within me.

This was my moment before the Seat of Judgment, in the Holy Tribunal of God. The spiritual presence of sin before the this tribunal is the greatest pain a soul could ever suffer. It is unspeakable and beyond compare. I found myself in a territory of evil so great that I lost all hope of seeing the light ever again. I experienced my own personal judgment, and my sentence was eternal damnation.

At death, when the soul faces its own personal judgment, it will find nothing that is unknown. Self-knowledge has already been infused in the person through the workings of the Holy Spirit. It is sin that causes this wisdom to lie dormant. In the presence of the Lord, the soul knows truth instantaneously.

The only confusion the soul experiences at the moment of physical death is the encounter with its relationship with evil. This takes it by surprise.

If, while on earth, we knew with clarity that we were in a hierarchical territory of sin, we would never allow ourselves to be deceived or manipulated and turned into such absurd puppets of Satan.

There is no half-way before the Judgment Seat of God. We cannot say we were sort of good or sort of bad. The dividing line disappears, and we are left either on one side or the other, destined for purgatory or heaven—or for hell.

I stood on evil ground. The devil had been my master, and on his terrain, I was to render an account to my Lord. In the Divine Presence, I was like a married man caught by his wife in his lover's embrace, unfaithful and in bed with the evil one for thirty-three years. I assumed that I would be in hell for an eternity, never to see the light of God again.

Suddenly, I was back on the mountain with my face on the grass. It seemed as though I'd never left this place of perfect silence, had never experienced hell, and yet, I knew I had.

Then Jesus began to speak to me again. As I was looking around, trying to discover where his voice was coming from, I found myself submerged up to my waist in a small lake.

Besides being acutely conscious of my presence in three different states—in the cave with the bats, lying down on the grass, and now in the lake—I was also made keenly aware of the relationship between each state. I know that this will seem as inconceivable to the reader as it seemed to me.

With my attention present in the dimension where I stood waist-deep in the lake, I looked up with my arms outstretched. There, in front of the lake, appeared an immense and precious golden rock, impossible to describe. It seemed to be as big as the universe. While unimaginable in size, my intellect could still fathom it.

In that same instant, I was made aware of myriads of evil spirits present in the lake. Then my guardian angel appeared on top of the rock. He was wearing a pale ivory tunic the same color as his face, as if it were part of his body.

With perfect knowledge, I knew everything he was saying without actually hearing him.

"You are standing in the territory of all of your sins," he said. "You lived your life against the commandments of God Almighty."

As he stared at the spirits of evil around me, his eyes were like torches of fire.

I was then shown my guardian angel's presence throughout my life, along with the presence of many other angels, including those of my relatives, or of people I had hurt, and I saw how the actions of those angels had been negated by my sins. I watched their spiritual struggle against the fallen spirits. It was devastating to see how many graces I had wasted and how much of my life I had spent with demons with so little awareness of them!

There was something even greater in this grand apparition, and I knew what it was: the Lord Himself.

Having only heard his voice up to this point, I understood that I was about to see him. In shame, I wanted to disappear into the lake. But he gave me the strength to look up at the pinnacle of the rock.

Very softly, smoothly, the Lord Jesus began to take shape as a person, transparent and immersed in majestic light. This revelation astounded me because for decades I had not thought of God as a divine person, but only as a vague cosmic energy or nirvana.

I melted into his presence, and his aura penetrated me so completely that I felt as if I were united to him. No words can describe my encounter with our king. I saw all of my life in him. I saw all of creation in him.

I would have expected to see him dressed in a tunic, but I can only say that he was dressed in the most precious light. At the same time, the most spectacular spectrum of colors as could delight the eyes appeared within him, presenting him in different accents of light.

These colors were like living creatures because of the enormous animation in which they existed. There is no comparison between the light and the colors I saw and what we see in the material world.

Jesus' hair was shoulder length and appeared in various shades of gold, from darkest to lightest. I was seeing him older and younger, all at the same time, with a face that was eternally beautiful, wise, powerful, and filled with infinite love.

I could not help but submerge myself completely in his eyes, which embodied unbridled love and compassion. They changed from yellow to blue to green, colors that caressed, bringing the greatest relief a soul could desire. To see the eyes of Jesus Christ is to find the absolute realization, the ultimate fulfillment, of our existence.

Our Lord was the resplendent mansion through which I could see heaven. Within him, I was witnessing an amazing, endless ocean of purity—a vast expanse of exquisite green. As my eyes focused on one particular spot, I realized that, like a green field is made up of millions of blades of grass, so was this ocean comprised of great numbers of individual angels and saints.

Then in the midst of the most colorful light, as if coming from the hearts of all the angels and saints, emerged the most splendid of all creatures, the Blessed Virgin Mary. She was precious and young and filled with such regal authority of abundant humility and grace that I was not able to stare at her.

Then I found myself like a child in her womb, connected to her through a spiritual umbilical cord. In the embrace of her being, I felt such tender nourishment that I was afraid to lose her. Together, she and all of the heavenly hosts began praising and worshiping the Lord in a single choir, which cannot be described in human terms. The presence of such perfection can only produce in the soul a state of sublime ecstasy.

My initial understanding of Jesus and Mary was so poor that every discovery was a profound one. I had never learned my catechism or paid attention in religion classes. The greatest of all revelations was to learn that Jesus Christ was God.

Moreover, to discover that I had a mother in heaven filled a profound maternal emptiness in my soul, a void which I was not aware of until the moment I saw her. While nestled as a child in her womb, I also remained waist deep in the lake. She spoke to me with profound love, in words I did not hear but understood perfectly:

"You have to trust in your Lord Jesus. You have to open your heart to let him in. Jesus loves you. He forgives you."

In my heart, however, it still felt impossible to accept the Lord's forgiveness because I was not able to forgive myself.

While I was with Our Lady, I was shown a large valley of loneliness, packed with millions of souls, which looked like a great body of fire, yet was as cold as ice.

It looked like hell, but my guardian angel told me I was seeing Purgatory, far below the earth. The souls in this state, he explained, had made it to salvation, but not to sainthood, so they had to be purified.

These souls were suffering because they were separated from God, whom they loved. In their spiritual senses, they were experiencing the extreme sensations of fire and ice, for it was either too hot or too cold.

The levels of purification in Purgatory were so many and so large that if a hundred people were to die suddenly and go there, they would not even be able to see each other. They would probably end up on different levels, according to their greater or lesser sins.

Our Lady, who is the queen of Purgatory, was feeling great compassion for each soul and never stopped interceding for them. She, my guardian angel, and other angels of the Lord were showing me how the souls I was seeing enjoy a beautiful and real assurance that they were saved. They accepted they could not yet attend the banquet of the Lord since they were not properly dressed in virtue, and they took great comfort in God's promise to them of heaven.

The Blessed Mother and the angels wanted me to accept that same mercy and hope for myself, but I could not.

I felt so unworthy that I turned my head away and looked down at the lake. Gently pursuing me, Mary met me on the surface of the water. Alongside her reflection, she pointed to the spirits of my sins and told me in a voice of the sweetest tenderness, "They are not you."

Finally, I was able to allow the Lord's mercy to envelope me. It was then that he began to lead me through extensive teachings. Jesus spoke about my life, humanity, the Church, the seven sacraments, the Ten Commandments, the Blessed Mother, the saints, heaven, purgatory, hell, demons, angels, eschatology, salvation, capital sins, and something he called the soul's economy, and so much more.

The state I was in is difficult to describe. The only way I can think to express this phenomenon would be to say that everything Jesus spoke of materialized in front of my eyes and was infused into my heart.

Words do not allow me to even approach the perfection, peace, and absolute wisdom in which his teachings took place, and I will never be able to measure them.

If I were to live another hundred years, I would not be able to convey even the minimum of all the Lord shared. I had never studied or read anything of what he taught me in books nor heard it from the people around me.

Everything was new.

✟   ✟   ✟

My entire mystical experience lasted throughout the night for about eight or nine hours. Then the Lord returned me to my physical body. As I reentered the prison of my flesh, my body went into convulsions.

Outwardly, I was back in the same living nightmare in the cave. Inwardly, I was an absolutely changed human being.

I lived in captivity for another five months. I suffered daily physical and psychological torture from the rebels, who were trying to get money out of me and my family. During those long months, I went through great suffering and desperation.

Never did I dream of making it out alive. I would look at those young men, knowing that they were prisoners of the devil. They were attacking me, physically and mentally, and they didn't know why. I felt so bad for them.

Every day I offered each suffering for the reparation of my sins. I now fully believed in God's mercy, but I was afraid of myself, of what I was going to do in the presence of the Lord again when I died. I begged him to send me someone who could give me Confession, even if it was a priest who had been kidnapped.

By the fourth month of my captivity, after I had given the FARC guerrillas every penny I had ever saved, it was much less than they wanted. They informed me they were awaiting instructions for my execution.

For the next couple of months, I lived waiting to be killed at any moment. Whenever I saw one of the men carrying a rope, it meant they were going to hang me. When I caught one sharpening a knife, I braced myself to be stabbed to death. If one was cleaning a machine gun, I anticipated getting shot to death. At least two times a day, I experienced, emotionally, my final moments of life.

One day a guerrilla rebel told me to ask the commandant to kill me on the road so that my family could find me. I followed his suggestion and approached the commandant.

"Could you kill me on the road?" I asked.

"No," he said. "We have to kill you in the jungle. I don't have time to take you to the road."

After that, I anticipated being murdered at any moment. One morning at 2:00 am, in the midst of torrential rain, I was untied from the tree to which I had been bound and ordered to follow four guerrillas. Through the early hours of the morning and into the rest of that weary day, they led me through one of Columbia's western rainforests—a dark, mountainous, and forbidding jungle.

By this point I was as thin as a rake, with a beard down to the center of my chest, still wearing the same ripped clothes that had been soaked in bat excrement six months earlier. For an entire half year, I had not slept in a bed or taken a shower.

After the sun emitted its final rays, we came to an unpaved road. The date was six months to the day of my kidnapping.

"Walk straight and don't look back," one of the guerrillas told me without explanation.

So I set forth with difficulty, my legs almost paralyzed by fear—with each step awaiting the ominous sound of a rifle shot piercing me and the dark, silent night. I begged God to let the bullet hit me in the head so I would be killed instantly, rather than left to suffer an agonizing death, mortally wounded on a lonely, secluded road.

It was the longest walk of my life. Petrified, I walked… and walked… and walked.

And nothing happened.

Approaching a curve in the road, I mustered the courage to glance behind me. Utterly confounded, I saw the four men climb back up the mountain in the direction of the woods from which we had come.

Could I dare hope? Would I be intercepted further down the road? My heart beat rapidly as I scanned the horizon in the faint moonlight, looking for rebels. But none appeared.

I had been kidnapped for so long that I didn't know what to do. I had lost my will. I actually started hoping the criminals would come back to tell me where to go and how to manage.

After what felt like hours, I heard the sound of a far-off engine. Along the dirt road came an old bus, which passed by on my left and stopped a few meters ahead of me.

A woman stepped off onto the dirt road and walked into the woods, and I realized she was one of the guerrillas.

Filled with adrenaline, I rushed to get to the door, which was shut in my face because I looked like a caveman. Shoving my elbow and knee in the crack of the door, I pried it open and stepped inside.

Everyone on the bus immediately turned their heads to look at me. Eyeing the empty, far-rear seat covered in broken glass and dust, I walked to the back of the bus and sat squarely in the center of the seat.

Through the rearview mirror, the driver stared, undoubtedly expecting me to do something terrible. I stared back at him. Everyone on the bus had swiveled their heads, looking at me.

Are they guerrillas, too? I asked.

I wondered if this was a setup. Even though I didn't know where I was, I didn't dare ask anyone anything. Somewhere inside my fear, I began to hope.

After a while, I made it to a town, then another. The police came around and my sisters eventually picked me up.

Our reunion was dramatic. They were ecstatic, and at the same time, pained to see me because I could not handle their expressions of love and affection.

After six months of being crushed, beaten, tied with rope, and undernourished, I was paranoid. There was no strength in me to receive a hug or a look of love because I had been punished every minute of every day with no conceivable end in sight but my murder. Cruelty was all I knew, so when my sisters came toward me, I felt scared. When they tried to grab me, my body shook and trembled.

They took me home, and I spent fifteen days locked in a bedroom. Unable to sit with anyone, I would inch my way to the table to eat on my own, making sure no one was around. When I needed to bathe, I could scarcely make my dash to the shower and back.

My sisters offered me psychiatric counseling, but I did not accept it. Only slowly did I begin to take little steps back into the world. It was easy, however, for me to pray—and pray. I knew that the Lord was going to heal me.

After I recuperated enough, physically and emotionally, the first thing I did was to go to Confession at a monastery in town. After standing in a long line, I found myself face-to-face with the abbot, a holy Franciscan with a long beard.

He listened kindly to my interminable confession.

Because we were in a room without furniture, my words echoed outside the confessional box, so the ladies waiting outside in line could hear my sins.

Finally I reached the end.

The priest said, "I'm going to give you absolution now…"

"God the Father of mercies, through the death and resurrection of his Son has reconciled the world to himself and sent the Holy Spirit among us for the forgiveness of sins. Through the ministry of the Church, may God give you pardon and peace, and I absolve you from your sins, in the name of the Father, and of the Son, and the Holy Spirit."

Feeling incredibly light and deliriously happy, I waved at everyone when I walked out. I could have confessed my sins in front of a million people because the Lord told me that sin is the devil and that we are all sinners.

Since I understood what had just happened mystically, I rejoiced in having hauled the devil off to jail. I could almost hear him and his legions being burned, one after the other.

Not only that, I was practically healed of all my paranoia and of every emotional and psychological consequence of my trauma from the kidnapping. It was the greatest sense of relief and deliverance of my entire life.

Shortly after that, I moved back to my home in California. The first thing I did was go back to the practice of faith.

My first experience of Holy Communion was a glimpse of heaven. Jesus overcame me in a way that is impossible to describe. How in love I was with the Lord and the Church, with the Scriptures, the Catechism, the liturgy, the stories of the saints!

Everything confirmed for me what I had learned through my mystical experience in the cave. To know that I was in the Church of the Lord, the House of God, made me feel so safe. Every day, I made sure to attend Mass, and began going to Confession often. I was home.

At church I felt shy around people because I was a Catholic who didn't even know the Our Father. When standing next to people in conversation about the faith, I would bend toward them to listen in. Sometimes they would become intimidated by this leaning stranger and stop speaking.

I joined prayer groups but kept silent about my mystical experience, never telling anyone, not even my sons. I figured it was a big secret between me and God, one that meant God was giving me another chance. I never considered that anyone would believe me anyway.

Although now spiritually fulfilled, I still felt devastated and exhausted from the kidnapping and the beatings. I did not think I would live much longer. All I wanted to do was move to a small town in northern Italy, retire, and live out my last few days in a simple, little, humble existence.

My family and friends were concerned about my strange behavior because I had stopped most of my former activities and was always in Church.

At age forty-nine, after two years living in Los Angeles, I made a trip back to Colombia during Holy Week. On Palm Sunday, I attended a noon Mass that was so packed I didn't make it inside. Through the main doors of the church, I peered above a sea of people and focused on a gigantic crucifix hanging above the altar. I began to feel dizzy, as if I might faint. Then I realized that the Lord was bringing me into another mystical experience.

He manifested himself again, this time from the crucifix, in the same way he had appeared to me on the rock. Whether I entered into the crucifix, or the crucifix entered into me, I do not know.

In this inexplicable state, the Lord showed me that my mission in this life was just about to begin. He said he was going to take me all around the world and that the knowledge he had infused into my soul was for me to share. He would support me and express himself through my testimony, using natural means—my speaking style, culture, and the languages I knew.

He told me that he had already chosen every place I would go, and chosen by name every person who was going to listen to me, adding that they would be responsible for everything I would tell them. The Lord's only immediate request of me was to be faithful, to pray, and to read the Word of God.

I didn't understand a thing he was communicating to me.

"No way," I told him. "So a sinner like me who has lived such a decadent life, persecuted the Church, and laughed at Christians and priests—I'm supposed to speak to a group and say, 'Hey, I sinned against the Lord, and then the Lord spoke to me?' I'll be greeted by tomatoes and rocks!"

Walking away from that Palm Sunday service, I thought, *Now I've really lost it.*

But the Lord had a plan. Recalling the holy abbot at the monastery who had heard my confession two years earlier, I returned to him again for Confession. I told him what the Lord had just told me, and disclosed my mystical encounter in the cave for the first time.

"Well, if everything you told me is from God, don't worry, Just go back home to California and he will take care of it."

What? I left there even more confused. I was hoping for an instruction manual.

But the abbot was right. A mysterious mission opened up before me. Though I had no idea that people gave testimonies in churches, I began to share my story in prayer groups and little gatherings.

That ignited a fire. Word of me spread everywhere, and I grew very scared. People started looking for me, and when I gave talks, they would pull out recorders and cameras, which I found disturbing.

Working for the Lord started to take all my time. My two sons, grown men, were independent, and my estranged wife had died long before, so I had no excuse not to follow God's call. The Lord had not allowed me to make my money back in Hollywood. He kept me as I was after my release from the kidnapping—poor and stripped.

Invitation after invitation poured in even though I never promoted myself. I became an international missionary and at the Lord's request founded a mission in 1999 called Pilgrims of Love with the Archdiocese of Bogotá. I have ecclesiastical approval from the Catholic Church, as prescribed in canon law. The first year of my mission was difficult. I lived out of a suitcase, traveling from place to place, diving headfirst into the incredible ocean of the Church.

Over the next four years, the Lord sent me to twenty-one countries and five continents! I have spoken at retreat centers, universities, high schools, seminaries, religious communities, Catholic parishes, Protestant churches, and so on.

I wondered, *How on earth am I going to support myself?*

But I have never lacked for anything, even at the eleventh hour, when I had no idea how the Lord would provide. I have never and will never charge for my talks. I live as Saint Paul did, on the generosity of the people. Paul built tents and I develop materials, writing books and recording talks. I live on faith.

As of today, I have written nine books and developed over a thousand different topics covering little windows of my mystical experience. Because the Lord walked me through so many different areas of the faith, I haven't come close to scratching the surface of what he infused in me.

I never studied theology or the religious sciences. I never prepared myself for this life. When I am about to give a talk, I never think ahead of time about what I will say—I leave it up to the Holy Spirit.

I am not special. You have read who I am. I was one of the most terrifying sinners. So why did the Lord pick me?

Because of his great mercy, and because he wants to make sure that those who hear or read of my experience know that the teachings I speak of come from him, not me. It is the Holy Spirit who shares them. It is as simple as that.

For me, I am begging the Lord not to let me die until I walk the last mile trying to repair all the damage I caused when I was living in mortal sin. Even if God were to give me a hundred years to do his work, I wouldn't feel completely at peace and ready to see him.

To speak and rescue souls from going to purgatory, and more importantly, from ending up in hell, is my desire until the day that the Lord calls me home.

What to Do Next

by Bud and Xavier Macfarlane

As you just experienced in the profound true stories in this book, the illumination of conscience is real. Every reader has a unique personal reaction to this information. It is perfectly normal to wonder what to do next. We respectfully offer the following helpful suggestions, beginning with your relationship to Jesus' visible church on earth.

If you were raised as a member of the Catholic Church, even if only as an infant by baptism, reunion is as simple as walking through a door. The first step is to attend Mass every Sunday, if it is available in your area.

Before receiving the Eucharist, as Jesus himself requested in the testimonies, make a sincere Confession. Begin deepening your prayer life, especially with the Holy Rosary. (If you don't know the Rosary, we will help you learn how to pray it at the end of this chapter.)

You can use the Internet to find a nearby Catholic parish. Contact a local priest to arrange for Confession or simply go at the times listed on MassTimes.org. Resources in the back of this book will help you prepare.

If you are not a formal member of the Catholic Church, consider becoming one. Most Catholic churches provide helpful classes to prepare new members in an orderly, beautiful way. In the United States this is called the Rite of Christian Initiation. Formally entering the Church may be accomplished more quickly and informally, so ask for guidance at the parish.

If you are a Protestant and were properly baptized, you are a member of the Mystical Body of Christ and are considered a "separated" brother or sister by the Catholic Church, even if you are not a formal member. We respect your love for Jesus, the Bible, and the Holy Spirit. You unknowingly already agree with Catholic teaching on many issues.

We humbly invite you to begin by prayerfully considering

becoming a Catholic because you want *more Jesus*. Because you desire *the fullness* of the truth. Come all the way home because you crave the certainty of absolution in Confession.

You are closer than you might realize. Many of our closest friends have made this exciting journey. (Our free recording, *The Conversion of Scott Hahn*, available at CatholiCity.com, is a wonderful place to begin.)

If you are in an eastern or orthodox church which broke away from the primacy of the papacy a long time ago, then prayerfully consider returning to unity. The Western Church has acknowledged its own human error in these complicated disputes while much progress toward reconciliation has been made in recent times.

As you may already know, there are twenty-three eastern and orthodox rites in communion with Rome which preserve your beautiful liturgies, architecture, traditions, sublime art, profound music, and family culture. You can find the right one for you and your family online.

✛ ✛ ✛

The people who shared their stories recounted the horrifying impact of evil spirits. Jesus Christ spoke frequently of demons in the Bible and cast them out to save people. As God, he has complete dominion over them, so be not afraid.

The witnesses in this book attest that serious sin invites demonic entities into our lives. Because eternal salvation is at stake, there will be a spiritual battle over your destiny when you seek to return or convert to Catholicism.

Expect to face unusual barriers and frustrations. Your car may break down on the way to Confession, your cell phone might become glitchy, or your boss, spouse, or friends might inadvertently throw up roadblocks. There will be emotional and psychological barriers, too, as you encountered through the testimonies in this book.

Be patient and loving if this occurs. Hang in there because these are signals that a battle for your soul is indeed taking place, and in the spiritual realm, this is good news. God is fighting *for you*. The Holy Spirit *will* help you.

Spiritual battles require spiritual strategies. This is why it is important to remove occult or New Age objects from our homes and to turn away from occult practices.

Replace these objects and images with sacred Catholic art, crucifixes, scapulars and Christian prayer. Sprinkle your home, car, and workplace with Holy Water (water blessed by a priest, usually available at most Catholic churches).

God has also given you a tireless spiritual bodyguard and companion—your very own guardian angel. Many people recite this traditional Catholic prayer daily:

Angel of God, my guardian dear, to whom God's love commits me here, ever this day be at my side, to light and guard, to rule and guide. Amen.

Remember, unseen evil entities will attempt to discourage you and sway you to procrastinate until you forget all about this book. The Kingdom of God consists not only of the people on earth, but of every soul in heaven, and you have, in great likelihood, relatives going back throughout history actively praying for you via their own union with God.

Rest assured that the saints in heaven played a part in this profound book coming into your life. Millions of people on earth, Catholics all over the world, have been praying for you every day.

You matter. You are never alone.

Please, too, rely on Saint Michael, the powerful archangel who cast the rebellious Satan out of heaven. We invite you to pray this prayer composed by Pope Leo XIII. Please pray it now and often:

Saint Michael the Archangel, defend us in battle, be our protection against the wickedness and snares of the devil. May God rebuke him, we humbly pray, and do thou, O Prince of the Heavenly Host, by the power of God, cast into hell Satan and all the evil spirits who prowl throughout the world seeking the ruin of souls. Amen.

As the testimonies you just read confirm, Jesus' Sacred Heart is burning with love for you no matter where you are and no matter what you are facing in life.

He wants to offer you his Divine Mercy. Seeking a deep daily connection with him through prayer, the sacramental life, praying the Rosary, and through relationships with other faithful Catholics is your path to happiness.

In addition to what we have already shared above, three free booklets we offer from the Mary Foundation are specially designed to help you get you started:

Seven Daily Habits for Faithful Catholics
Powerful Prayers Every Catholic Should Know
Going Back to Confession After Years or Decades.

Read them online or order free copies at CatholiCity.com.

Be sure to order or stream our free recording, *The Rosary and Divine Mercy Chaplet.* As the most popular audio Rosary in history, it has helped many millions learn how to pray the Holy Rosary and fall in love with Mary.

Like this very book, it is our free gift to you. And if you are like most readers, the Holy Spirit will inspire you to share this extraordinary little book with others.

Welcome to our work!

These and many other helpful resources are available from Queen of Peace Media and the Mary Foundation.

Jesus Christ is your king, your savior, your brother, and your friend. Living life with him brings inner peace, awareness of supernatural realities, strength during difficult times, profound joy, power to overcome sin, divine help in matters great and small, and unexpected blessings—not only *for you*, but *through you* for your family, everyone you love, and for the countless people God wants you to help.

As you witnessed in Marino Restrepo's amazing story, Jesus declared that He already knew *every* person Marino would touch in the future.

You are now one of those people.

Prophecies of the Warning

by Christine Watkins

What is the Warning?

A variety of independent sources provide details about the worldwide cosmic and spiritual event known as the Warning or the Illumination of Conscience. Jesus, the Mother of God, Blessed Pope Pius IX, Saint Edmund Campion, and many other mystics all teach us the Warning will be a direct intervention from God, a "great wonder, which will fill the world with astonishment."[1] "It will be terrible, a Mini-Judgment."[2] God will "reveal all men's consciences and try every man of each kind of religion."[3]

First, a terrible darkness will obscure the sun's light. Even the stars and the moon will fail to shine. The dome of the sky will be illuminated by an apparent collision of two celestial bodies, producing a powerful booming noise. The days will be brighter and nights will shine like day.

Then Jesus will appear in the sky on his Cross—not in his suffering, but in his glory. This sign of the Lord will be visible everywhere. Brilliant rays of love and mercy proceeding from the five wounds of his pierced hands, feet, and side will illuminate the entire world.

These rays will contain the Blessed Mother's "Flame of Love" which leaps out to souls. "Due to lack of faith, the earth is entering into darkness, but earth will experience a great jolt of faith,"[4] Our Lady revealed to Elizabeth Kindelmann.

---

1 Concerning the prophetic words of St. Pope Pius IX: Rev. R. Gerald Culleton, *The Prophets and Our Times* (Tan Books and Publishers, 1941), p. 206.

2 RE: the Church-approved apparitions at Heede, Germany. D. Alfonso Cenni, *I SS. Cuori di Gesu e di Maria. La Salvezza del Mondo. Le Loro Apparizioni, Promesse e Richieste. Nihil Obstat* Ex Parte Ordinis Il P. Generale D. Pier-Damiano Buffadini, February 24, 1949. *Imprimatur* Sublaci. Simon Laurentius O.S.B. Ep, tit. Abb. Ord. June 3, 1949.

3 Evelyn Waugh, *Two Lives: Edmund Campion and Ronald Knox* (Continuum; 2005), p. 113.

4 Elizabeth Kindelmann, *The Flame of Love* (Children of the Father Foundation; 2015-2016) *Nihil Obstat:* Monsignor Joseph G. Prior, Censor Librorum. *Imprimatur:* Archbishop Charles Chaput, Archdiocese of Philadelphia, p. 61.

Our Lady explained further:

> In that dark night, heaven and earth will be illuminated
> by the Flame of Love that I offer to souls.[5]
>   It is so great that I cannot keep it any longer within
> me. It leaps out to you with explosive power. When it
> pours out, my love will destroy the satanic hatred that
> contaminates the world. The greatest number of souls
> will be set free. Nothing like this has existed before. This
> is my greatest miracle that I will do for all.[6]

Everything will stop when the Warning occurs. Every person
and every activity on earth will freeze in time and space. Yet
in the ensuing five to fifteen minutes, all people, religious
or atheist, mentally incapacitated or sane, young or old, will
see the sinfulness of their lives. As you have just read in the
many testimonies in this book, everyone will see the evil they
have done and the good they have failed to do. The Cross will
remain visible in the skies for seven days and seven nights.
    From the early past century to the present day, heaven has
provided more information about this unparalleled event. In
1934 Jesus spoke to Saint Maria Faustina Kowalska regarding
the nature of the Warning:

> All light in the heavens will be extinguished and there
> will be great darkness over the whole earth. Then the sign
> of the Cross will be seen in the sky, and from the holes
> where the hands and the feet of the Savior were nailed
> will come forth a brilliant light, which will illuminate the
> earth for a period of time.[7]

In the Gospel, Jesus describes the Warning:

> Immediately after the tribulation of those days, the sun
> will be darkened, and the moon will not give its light,
> and the stars will fall from the sky, and the powers of the

---

5   Ibid., p. 62.
6   Ibid., pp. 44-45.
7   Saint Maria Faustina Kowalska, *Divine Mercy in My Soul: Diary* (Marian Press,
    3rd Edition; 2003) #83.

heavens will be shaken. And then the sign of the Son of Man will appear in heaven, and all the tribes of the earth will mourn, and they will see the Son of Man coming upon the clouds of heaven with power and great glory. And he will send out his angels with a trumpet blast, and they will gather his elect from the four winds, from one end of the heavens to the other. (Matthew 24: 29-31)

The Warning is also described in the Book of Revelation:

Then I watched while he broke open the sixth seal, and there was a great earthquake; the sun turned as black as dark sackcloth and the whole moon became like blood. The stars in the sky fell to the earth like unripe figs shaken loose from the tree in a strong wind. Then the sky was divided like a torn scroll curling up, and every mountain and island was moved from its place.

The kings of the earth, the nobles, the military officers, the rich, the powerful, and every slave and free person hid themselves in caves and among mountain crags. They cried out to the mountains and the rocks, "Fall on us and hide us from the face of the one who sits on the throne and from the wrath of the Lamb, because the great day of their wrath has come and who can withstand it?" (Rev 6: 12-17)

In 1945 in Heede, Germany, Jesus said that when the Mini-Judgment comes, "The Earth will shake and moan."[8] In 2014 Jesus told the mystic Luz de María de Bonilla:

My beloved people, the examination of your consciences will come soon… Whatever moves will stop moving, for silence will reign on earth. You will hear only the lamentations of those repenting for the wrongs they committed, and I will come with my love to once again welcome my lost sheep.[9]

---

8 Ibid., Cenni, *I SS. Cuori*, Imprimatur Sublaci. Simon Laurentius O.S.B.
9 Luz de María de Bonilla, *Venga a Nosotros Tu Reino* ("*Thy Kingdom Come*") Year 2014, with the *Imprimatur* and full support of Juan Abelardo Mata Guevara, SDB, Titular Bishop of Estelí, Nicaragua.

Prophecies of the Warning in Our Times

One of the earliest historical accounts of the Warning comes from Saint Edmund Campion, the brilliant sixteenth-century Jesuit priest and martyr from England, who wrote:

> I pronounced a great day, not wherein any temporal potentate should minister, but wherein the Terrible Judge should reveal all men's consciences and try every man of each kind of religion.[10]

This saint's prophecy foreshadows the numerous prophecies to follow. Two centuries later, God revealed the Warning to the Italian mystic, Blessed Anna Maria Taigi.

Paupers, priests, and popes alike sought advice from this humble mother because she was given a remarkable mystical gift. For forty-seven years, a bright orb of light accompanied her day and night. She had but to gaze into it to see the secret thoughts of persons near and far, events of bygone days, and the details of days yet to come.

Her prophecies have withstood the test of time, and hers are the first to use the phrase *Illumination of Conscience*. "A great purification will come upon the world preceded by an Illumination of Conscience in which everyone will see themselves as God sees them."[11]

Why God is Sending the Warning

God will send the Warning in order to prevent souls from falling into hell. At Heede in the 1940s Jesus said:

> My love has planned this action before the creation of the world. People do not listen to my calls: they close their ears; they resist grace and reject my mercy, my love, my merits. The world is worse than before the deluge. It agonizes in a quagmire of sin. Hatred and greed have infiltrated human hearts. All this is the work of Satan. The world lies in dense darkness. This generation deserves to be wiped out, but I wish to show it my mercy. The cup of

---

10 Waugh, *Two Lives*, p. 113.
11 Iannuzzi, *Antichrist*, p. 33. Petrisko, *The Miracle*, p. 27.

God's anger is already spilling over onto the nations. The angel of peace will not delay in coming down to earth. I want to heal and save. Through the wounds that bleed now, mercy will win and justice triumph.[12]

In 1980, the Lord said to Elizabeth Kindelmann, "The Church and the whole world are in danger. You cannot change this situation. Only the Holy Trinity, through the unified intercession of the Blessed Virgin, the angels, the saints, and the souls in purgatory, can help you."[13] Other prophets provide confirmation: "The very fact that such judgments will come is because people refuse to convert and continue to live in darkness,"[14] Jesus revealed to Janie Garza. "Humanity must be purified so that it does not fall into the flames of hell,"[15] Our Lady told Luz de María.

In 2018, God the Father gave this message to Fr. Michel Rodrigue, mystic, abbot, and founder of the Apostolic Fraternity of Saint Benedict Joseph Labre:

I do not want death and damnation for any one of you. So much suffering, so much violence, so many sins now occur on the earth that I created. I now hear the cries of all the babies and children who are murdered by the sin of my children who live under the dominion of Satan. *You shall not kill.*[16]

The Warning for People in Serious Sin

As in the lives you just read in this book, the Warning will be terrifying if you live a sinful life without God. Some will even die from the emotional trauma. "For those who are not in a state of grace, it will be frightening,"[17] Jesus warned at Heede.

---

12 Ibid., Cenni, *I SS. Cuori*, Imprimatur Sublaci. Simon Laurentius O.S.B.

13 Kindelmann, *The Flame*, p. 108.

14 Janie Garza, *Heaven's Messages for the Family: How to Become the Family God Wants You to Be* (Saint Dominic Media, 1998), p. 329.

15 Bonilla, *Venga*, with *Imprimatur* and full support of Juan Abelardo Mata Guevara, SDB, Titular Bishop of Estelí, Nicaragua, Message of March 5, 2013, p. 56.

16 From Fr. Michel Rodrigue's live recorded talk in Barry's Bay, Ontario, Canada, on July 12, 2018.

17 Ibid., Cenni, *I SS. Cuori*, *Imprimatur* Sublaci. Simon Laurentius O.S.B.

In the 1960s, in the mountain village of Garbandal, Spain, the Warning was allegedly described by Our Lady to four young girls. The visionary Conchita revealed that it will be:

> …a thousand times worse than earthquakes. It will be like fire; it will not burn our flesh; we will feel it corporeally and interiorly… And unbelievers will feel the fear of God. If we die during that time, it will be of fright… If I could only tell you how the Virgin described it to me![18]

"I speak of the Warning," said Jesus in 2018 to Luz de María de Bonilla, "…a moment so overpowering that some will not survive experiencing their own wickedness."[19]

Saint Joseph, the husband of Mary and the earthly father of Jesus, confided to Janie Garza in 1994, "For those who believe that they live in the light but continue to break every commandment given by God, to these souls, I, Saint Joseph, say that these souls will not be able to see the state of their souls *and live.*"

Janie responded, "Are you saying that people who do not live God's commandments will die when they see their souls?"

Saint Joseph then confirmed, "Yes, my little one, that's how it will be for many unless they repent and decide for conversion. There is still time for repentance, but time is growing shorter with each day that goes by."[20]

Fr. Rodrigue explained what God the Father revealed to him regarding souls destined for damnation:

> For the ones who would go to hell, they will burn. Their bodies will not be destroyed, but they will feel exactly what hell is like because they are already there. The only thing missing was the feeling. They will experience the beatings of the devil, and many will not survive because

18 Ramon Pérez, *Garabandal: The Village Speaks,* translated from the French by Matthews, Annette I. Curot, The Workers of Our Lady of Mount Carmel, 1981, pp. 50-51.

19 Bonilla, *Venga, Imprimatur*: Bishop Guevara, Revelaciones Marianas, p. 124,.

20 Janie Garza, *Heaven's Messages for the Family, Volume II: Messages from St. Joseph and the Archangels* (Saint Dominic Media, 1999), p. 46.

of their great sin, I assure you. But it will be for them a blessing, because they will ask for pardon. It will be their salvation.[21]

For Those in Friendship with God

When a friend of Conchita's shared that she was frightened by the prospect of the Warning, Conchita reassured her, "Yes, but after the Warning, you will love God much more."[22]

Another Garabandal visionary, Jacinta, declared, "The Warning is for us to draw closer to Him and to increase our faith. Therefore, one should prepare for that day, but not await it with fear. God does not send things for the sake of fear, but rather with justice and love."[23]

> Those who behave and act in my likeness toward their neighbor, and repent with all their strength, force, and feelings, and confess their sins with a firm purpose of amendment, those children of mine will experience the Warning like every human being will, but not with the intensity of those who stoop in the mire of sin through disobedience, ignoring my calls, those of my mother, and my faithful Saint Michael the Archangel.[24] (Jesus to Luz de María)

As foreshadowed in the testimonies in this book, each person will experience the Warning differently because no one has committed the same sins. According to Fr. Michel Rodrigue:

> For those who are very close to Jesus, they will see what they must change in order to live in complete union with him. The Father wants me to proclaim that you do not have to fear. For the one who believes in God, this will be a loving day, a blessed day. You will see what you must correct to accomplish more of his will, to be more

---

21 From Fr. Michel Rodrigue's live recorded talks in Barry's Bay, Ontario on July 12 and 13, 2018.

22 "Conchita and Loli Speak on the Aviso," Garabandal Journal, January-February 2004, p. 5.

23 Garabandal International Magazine, October-December, 2014.

24 Bonilla, *Venga*, Bishop Guevara, Revelaciones Marianas.

submissive to the grace he wishes to give you for your mission on earth.[25]

The Warning is Coming Soon

Throughout history, the precise timing of prophesied events has been unclear. Prophecies about a coming Messiah can be found hundreds of years before Jesus' incarnation and were recorded in the Old Testament as early as 1450 BC.

However, God has been announcing the Warning for the past five centuries with increasing frequency, urgency, and detail. We should keep in mind, however, as Saint Peter wrote, "…that with the Lord one day is like a thousand years." (2 Peter 3: 8b)

In 1945, Jesus said at Heede, "My beloved children, the hour is near… The angels of justice are now scattered across the world. I will make myself known to mankind. Every soul will recognize me as their God. I am coming!"[26]

In 1964, Mary told Elizabeth Kindelmann, "The moment is near when my Flame of Love will ignite."[27]

Jacinta of Garabandal adds that when the Warning comes, conditions will be "at their worst."

Her fellow visionary, Mari Loli, related that it will seem as if the Church had disappeared: "…it will be very hard to practice the religion, for priests to say Mass, or for people to open the doors of the churches."

In 1975, Mari Loli added, "All I can say is that it is very near, and that it is very important that we get ready for it."[28]

In 1995, Jesus told Janie Garza that the Warning…

> …will happen within a short period. Do not be distracted with dates, but prepare every day with strong prayer. Many who worry about these times will not live to see these

25 Fr. Michel Rodrigue's live recorded talks.

26 Ibid., Cenni, *I SS. Cuori, Imprimatur* Sublaci. Simon Laurentius O.S.B.

27 Elizabeth Kindelmann, *The Flame of Love of the Immaculate Heart of Mary: The Spiritual Diary, Imprimatur:* Cardinal Péter Erdo, Archbishop of Budapest and Primate of Hungary (The Flame of Love Movement of the Immaculate Heart of Mary; Montreal, Canada) 2014, p. 61.

28 Ramon Pérez, *Garabandal: The Village Speaks,* translated from the French by Matthews, Annette I. Curot, The Workers of Our Lady of Mount Carmel, 1981, pp. 52.

things take place. This is why Holy Scripture warns everybody not to be concerned about tomorrow, for tomorrow is promised to no one. The present day has enough trials and crosses. Know that when we speak about such things to come, this is for the people to convert and abandon their evil ways. Every day is an opportunity for souls to convert. People should not wait for such things to come to convert, but they should convert now, before it's too late.[29]

Heaven seems to be announcing that the Warning will occur in this generation. Words to both Luz de María and Fr. Rodrigue, whose messages are ongoing, appear especially urgent.

In 2010, Jesus told Luz de María de Bonilla, "My mother has announced throughout the whole world and across time what is now on the horizon." In 2013, Mary, the Mother of God, told her:

How close to this generation is to the Warning! And how many of you do not even know what the Warning is. In these times, my faithful instruments and my prophet are mocked by those who consider themselves scholars of spirituality, by those who reach millions of souls through means of mass communication. They are misleading them and hiding the truth because I am the one revealing the will of the Trinity, the will of the Trinity already expressed in all of my apparitions, starting from long ago.

In 2019, Saint Michael the Archangel declared to her, "This is the generation that will experience the great act of Divine Mercy: The Warning."[30]

How to Prepare for the Warning
At Heede, Jesus spoke with great vehemence regarding how one should prepare for the Warning:

29 Janie Garza, *Heaven's Messages for the Family: How to Become the Family God Wants You to Be* (Saint Dominic's Media, 1998).
30 "The Great Warning of God to Humanity: Prophecies and Revelations Given to Luz de María de Bonilla," Imprimatur of Bishop Guevara, Revelaciones Marianas.

Humanity has not listened to My Holy Mother, who appeared at Fatima to urge mankind to do penance. Now I, myself, have come to warn the world in this last hour: the times are serious! May people finally do penance for their sins; may they turn away with all their heart from evil and pray, pray much, in order to calm the indignation of God. May they often recite the Holy Rosary, in particular: this prayer is powerful with God. Less entertainments and amusements! I am very near.[31]

In 1966 Saint Joseph advised Janie Garza about preparation:

Pray, my little one, pray. Remain faithful to all that the Holy Spirit directs you to do. Act in everything that Most Holy Mary is calling you to. Be a strong messenger of living her messages of peace, prayer, Holy Mass, fasting, conversion, and reading Holy Scripture. Do this as a family. Do not reject God's Most Holy Name so that he will not reject you. Decide to be a holy family, to pray together, to love, and to forgive one another. This is a time of decision for all of God's children. Live as God's people, leading good, simple, and just lives.[32]

In summary, the prophecies recommend recourse to timeless Catholic practices of piety: frequent Confession, daily Mass, fasting, reading Holy Scripture, contemplative prayer, the Rosary, family prayer, Eucharistic adoration, and consecrating oneself and one's family to the Sacred Heart of Jesus and the Immaculate Heart of Mary.

What Will Happen After the Warning?
After people experience the Warning, they "will ache for not having believed," Mary explained to Luz de María. "But they will have already misled many of my children who will not be able to recuperate so easily, for the godless will deny the Warning and attribute it to new technologies."[33]

31 Cenni, I SS. Cuori, Imprimatur Sublaci. Simon Laurentius O.S.B.

32 Janie Garza, Heaven's Messages for the Family, Volume II: Messages from St. Joseph and the Archangels (Saint Dominic Media, 1999), pp. 201-202.

33 Bonilla, Venga, Imprimatur: Bishop Guevara, Revelaciones Marianas, p. 56.

Jesus also explained to her:

> My Cross is Victory, and it will shine in the firmament for seven days and nights. It will radiate light constantly. It will be a preliminary sign for which my people have waited. And for those who do not believe, there will be great confusion. Science will try to give an explanation for that which has no scientific explanation. ...Even then, some of my children will deny that the Warning came from my kingdom and will rebel against me, uniting with evil.[34]

According to Fr. Michel Rodrigue:

> God has not given us three ways to travel, only two. There is no grey area in between the path of evil and the path of the Lord. Those who will say, 'I don't know. I cannot make a decision,' will not be able to remain indifferent. As God says in the Book of Revelation, 'So, because you are lukewarm, neither hot nor cold, I will spit you out of my mouth.' People will have to make a decisive choice, and you will understand why because after that, they will be left with the consequences of their decision. The time of mercy will end, and the time of justice will begin. Jesus said this to Saint Faustina Kowalska.[35]

Therefore, as a special reprieve from God, during the Warning and for a short time afterward, Satan will be blinded and unable to tempt souls. Without this divine protection, souls would not be able to see the absolute truth of their state before God, nor have the complete freedom of will to choose God or reject Him.

There will be a great unification of the Kingdom of God. When asked what will happen to the many churches, Jacinta of Garabandal answered, "All humanity would be within one Church, the Catholic Church. She also said it was very important to pray for this intention."[36]

---

34 Ibid p. 290.
35 Fr. Michel Rodrigue's live recorded talks.
36 Interview with Jacinta conducted by Barry Hanratty April 16,1983, St. Michael's Garabandal Center for Our Lady of Carmel, Inc.

In the 1600s, Blessed Anna Maria Taigi was shown by God that entire nations would return to the unity of the Church. Many Muslims, pagans, and Jews would be converted.[37]

Confirming the worldwide "period of peace" promised in 1917 by Our Lady of Fatima, Saint Joseph described the new era to Janie Garza:

> There will be great joy for all the faithful people of God. His children will be happy. There will be love in families everywhere. People will benefit from their labor, and they will build their homes and live to enjoy them. They will see their children's children, and all will live long lives.[38]

Finally, Jesus also promised at Heede:

> I will come with my peace. I will build my kingdom with a small number of elect. This kingdom will come suddenly, sooner than men think... My beloved children, the hour is near. Pray unceasingly, and you will not be confused. I am gathering my elect. They will come together from every part of the world, and they will glorify me. I am coming![39]

ORDER CHRISTINE WATKINS' FULL-LENGTH VERSION!
The Warning
Testimonies and Prophecies of the Illumination of Conscience
(with the Imprimatur of the Catholic Church)

Six More Astounding Illumination of Conscience Testimonies
Extensive Scholarship about Prophecies of the Warning
Biographies of Prophets of the Warning
Extensive Photographs and End Notes
Foreword by Bishop Gavin Ashenden... and more

www.queenofpeacemedia.com

---

37 Mark Regis, "Blessed Anna-Maria Taigi," Garabandal Journal, January-February 2004, pp. 6-8.
   Albert Bessieres, SJ, translated from the French by Rev. Stephen Rigby, _Wife, Mother and Mystic_ (Tan Books, 1970).
38 Janie Garza, _Heaven's Messages for the Family: How to Become the Family God Wants You to Be_ (Saint Dominic Media, 1998), p. 201.
39 Cenni, _I SS. Cuori_, Imprimatur Sublaci. Simon Laurentius O.S.B.

Do you want to introduce this book to your...

Family

Friends

Social Networks

Prayer Group

Church or Parish

Business Associates

Local Bookstore Owner

Local School or Library

Pastor or Priest

For the extraordinarily small donation of only $1 each we will send you dozens, hundreds, or even thousands of copies—with free shipping! Use the convenient order form at the back of this book or order online today at:

www.catholicity.com

RESOURCES FROM QUEEN OF PEACE MEDIA

More Books by Christine Watkins
Of Men and Mary (Six Conversion Stories)
Full of Grace: Miraculous Stories of Healing
Transfigured: Patricia Sandoval's Story
Mary's Mantle Consecration: A Spiritual Retreat
She Who Shows the Way: Heaven's Messages
The Warning: Testimonies and Prophecies
Winning the Battle for Your Soul (Marino Restrepo)
In Love with True Love (Sister Nicolina Kohler)
The Flame of Love (Diary of Elizabeth Kindelmann)
Marie-Julie Jahenny: Prophecies for the End Times

For titles available in Spanish:
Please refer to our website

Online Resources
Radio Maria Weekly Show
Videos and Blogs
Prayer Requests and much more

For More on the Warning
CountdowntotheKingdom.com

Coming Soon from Balladream Films
TheWarningMovie.com

Follow Queen of Peace Media
YouTube
Facebook
Instagram
Pinterest

Order Online
www.queenofpeacemedia.com

FREE GIFTS FROM THE MARY FOUNDATION

Bestselling Novels by Bud Macfarlane
Pierced by a Sword
Conceived Without Sin
House of Gold

Booklets
Powerful Prayers Every Catholic Should Know
Going Back to Confession After Years or Decades
Seven Daily Habits for Faithful Catholics

Streaming Audio, CDs, and Podcasts
The Rosary and Divine Mercy Chaplet
Marian Apparitions Explained
Confession
The Mass Explained
Seven Secrets of the Eucharist
The Conversion of Scott Hahn
The Conversion of Roy Schoeman

Medals Touched to Relics of Saints with Prayer Cards
Miraculous Medal: with Consecration to Mary
True Cross Crucifix: with daily Adoration Prayer
Saint Joseph Medal: with Consecration to Joseph
Saint Benedict Medal: with Saint Michael Prayer

Sacred Objects, Images, and Spiritual Protection
Purple Scapular for protection during the End Times
Special Jerusalem Rosaries touched to the True Cross
Wall Crucifixes touched to the True Cross
Beautiful Images of the Mother of God

Order Online
www.catholicity.com

Powerful Daily Prayers

Morning Offering
Dear Lord, I do not know what will happen to me today—I only
know that nothing will happen that was not foreseen by you and
directed to my greater good from all eternity. I adore your holy
and unfathomable plans and submit to them will all my heart for
love you, the pope, and the Immaculate Heart of Mary, amen.

Act of Contrition
O my God, I am heartfully sorry for having offended thee, and
I detest all my sins because of they just punishment, but most
of all because I have offend thee, my God, who is all good
and deserving of all my love. I firmly resolve, with the help of thy
grace, to sin no more and to avoid the near occasion of sin, amen.

Saint Michael the Archangel Prayer
Saint Michael the Archangel, defend us in battle, be our
protection against the wickedness and snares of the devil.
May God rebuke him, we humbly pray, and do thou
O Prince of the Heavenly Host, by the power of God,
cast into hell Satan and all the evil spirits who prowl throughout
the world seeking the ruin of souls, amen.

Our Father
Our Father, who art in heaven, hallowed be thy name.
Thy kingdom come, thy will be done, on earth as it is in heaven.
Give us this day our daily bread and forgive us our trespasses
as we forgive those who trespass against us. Lead us not into
temptation but deliver us from evil, amen.

Hail Mary
Hail Mary, full of grace, the Lord is with thee. Blessed art thou
among women, and blessed is the fruit of thy womb, Jesus.
Holy Mary, Mother of God, pray for us sinners,
now and at the hour of our death, amen.

Total Consecration to Immaculate Mary
O Mary, conceived without sin, on this day I implore you to take
all that I am completely to yourself. Direct all my powers
of body and soul, from this moment forward, to whatever pleases
your divine Son. May this total consecration to your Immaculate
Heart inspire me to bring to you souls indifferent to God, and thus
help extend the kingdom of the most Sacred Heart of Jesus, amen.

Guardian Angel Prayer
Angel of God, my guardian dear, to whom God's love
commits me here, ever this day be at my side,
to light and guard, to rule and guide, amen.

The Jesus Prayer
Lord Jesus Christ, Son of the Living God,
have mercy on me, a sinner.

O My Jesus (Fatima Prayer)
O my Jesus, forgive us our sins, save us from the fires of hell.
Lead all souls to heaven, especially those
in most need of thy mercy, amen.

Glory Be
Glory be to the Father, and to the Son, and to the Holy Spirit,
as it was in the beginning, is now, and ever shall be,
world without end, amen.

Grace Before Meals
Bless us O Lord, and these thy gifts, which we are about
to receive, from thy bounty, though Christ Our Lord, amen.

Making the Sign of the Cross
Bring right hand to forehead, chest, left shoulder, then right, saying...
In the name of the Father, and of the Son,
and of the Holy Spirit, amen.

Acknowledgments

From the Mary Foundation
The editors offer our gratitude to Christine Watkins and
Queen of Peace Media for helping reach more people
through this free version of their original work.

From Queen of Peace Media
Special thanks to those who bravely shared their remarkable stories of undergoing an illumination of conscience,
and to William Underwood, Dan Osanna, Anne Manyak,
Linda Kline, and to Judy Dayton for lending their keen
eyes and golden hearts to the making of the original, full-
length version of this book.

Experience the Warning

Dear Reader,

   More than one million people have "lived through" the Warning in my father's award-winning novel, **Pierced by a Sword,** an immersive experience into the Coming Tribulations. The characters are unforgettable.

   Millions more have learned about the Warning in the riveting summary of messages from the Mother of God in a talk by my grandfather, Bud Macfarlane Sr., called *Marian Apparitions Explained.* It is one of the most popular Catholic recordings of all time by one of the world's leading experts.

   It can change your life.

   In the testimonies you just read, Jesus emphasized the importance of praying the Rosary. Our free recording, *The Rosary,* is a wonderful tool for learning how to pray it. It's also perfect for everyday use.

   The most popular Rosary recording in history, it also includes daily Catholic prayers, the Divine Mercy Chaplet, and a great talk about Mary from a former Protestant minister who became a Catholic. Stream it online or order the CD.

   These helpful resources *are all free:* for you, your family, and friends, so order online at CatholiCity.com or use the form on the back of this page to get started.

With Christ,

Xavier Macfarlane
The Mary Foundation
Editor, Concise Revised Edition

Order FREE Novels and CDs

Experience the Warning

(Please Print)

Name: _____

Address: _____

City: _____

State: _____ Zip: _____

Email: _____

For questions about your order and Bud Macfarlane's monthly email message.

Suggested **optional** donation for up to ten items: **$1 to $10 each.**
Minimum donation for **more than ten items: $1 to $5 each.**

Quantity **Pierced by a Sword Novel**	+	Quantity **Marian Apparitions CD**	+	Quantity **The Rosary CD**	=	Total **Number of Novels/CDs**
_____		_____		_____		_____

X Donation per Novel/CD $_____

= Gift for Novels/CDs $_____

Optional Gift for Shipping $_____
Canada, Other Countries: You must order online.
USA: Add $10 for faster Guaranteed Shipping.

Optional Gift to Support Our Work $_____

TOTAL DONATION $_____

CatholiCity.
FOR FASTEST DELIVERY
Order Online:
www.catholicity.com

Mary Foundation.
Mail this Form to:
The Mary Foundation
PO Box 26101 • Fairview Park, OH 44126

Outside the USA: Online orders only. Make checks payable to "The Mary Foundation"
Your gift is tax deductible. We'll ship your materials the day we receive your letter or online order.
We only send materials to those who write us directly: **do not** send us any address other than your own.

How the Mary Foundation Works

- We will send up to ten free books. A donation is optional. Free shipping.

- Fast Delivery. All requests will be shipped on the day we receive your order.

- We will not give your personal information to other organizations.

- Outside the United States: only online orders will be accepted. www.catholicity.com

- We only send materials to those who contact us directly. Do not send us any address of people other than yourself.

- We welcome your feedback and opinions. Typographical and grammar suggestions are appreciated (include page and line number).

- Bookstores, retailers, groups, schools, and other organizations: please refer to our website for bulk discounts and free promotional displays.

Thank you for being a part of our work!

Order FREE Warning Books

(Please Print)

Name: _____

Address: _____

City: _____

State: _____ Zip: _____

Email: _____
For questions about your order and Bud Macfarlane's monthly email message.

Suggested **optional** donation for up to ten books: **$1 to $10 each.**
Minimum donation for **more than ten books: $1 to $5 each.**

Quantity: **The Warning** by Christine Watkins _____

   X Donation per Book $ _____

   = Total Donation $ _____

Optional Gift for Shipping $ _____
Canada, Other Countries: You must order online.
USA: add $10 for faster Guaranteed Shipping.

Optional Gift to Support Our Work $ _____

TOTAL DONATION $ _____

CatholiCity.
FOR FASTEST DELIVERY
Order Online:
www.catholicity.com

Mary Foundation.
Mail this Form to:
The Mary Foundation
PO Box 26101 • Fairview Park, OH 44126

Outside the USA: Online orders only. Make checks payable to "The Mary Foundation"
Your gift is tax deductible. We'll ship your materials the day we receive your letter or online order.
We only send materials to those who write us directly: **do not** send us any address other than your own.